I just wanted to paint and sketch and tell stories by drawing.

ROBERT REDFORD

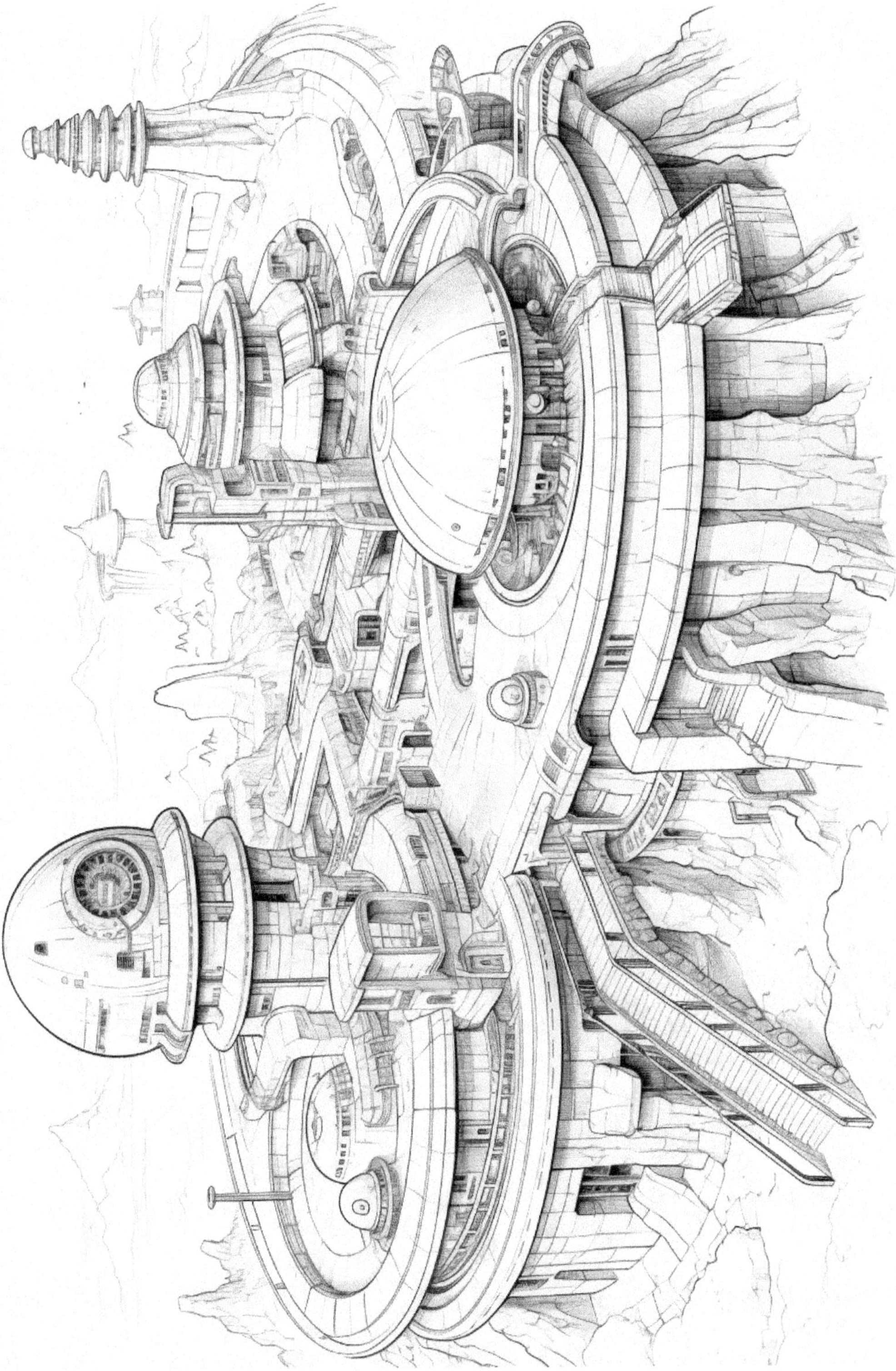

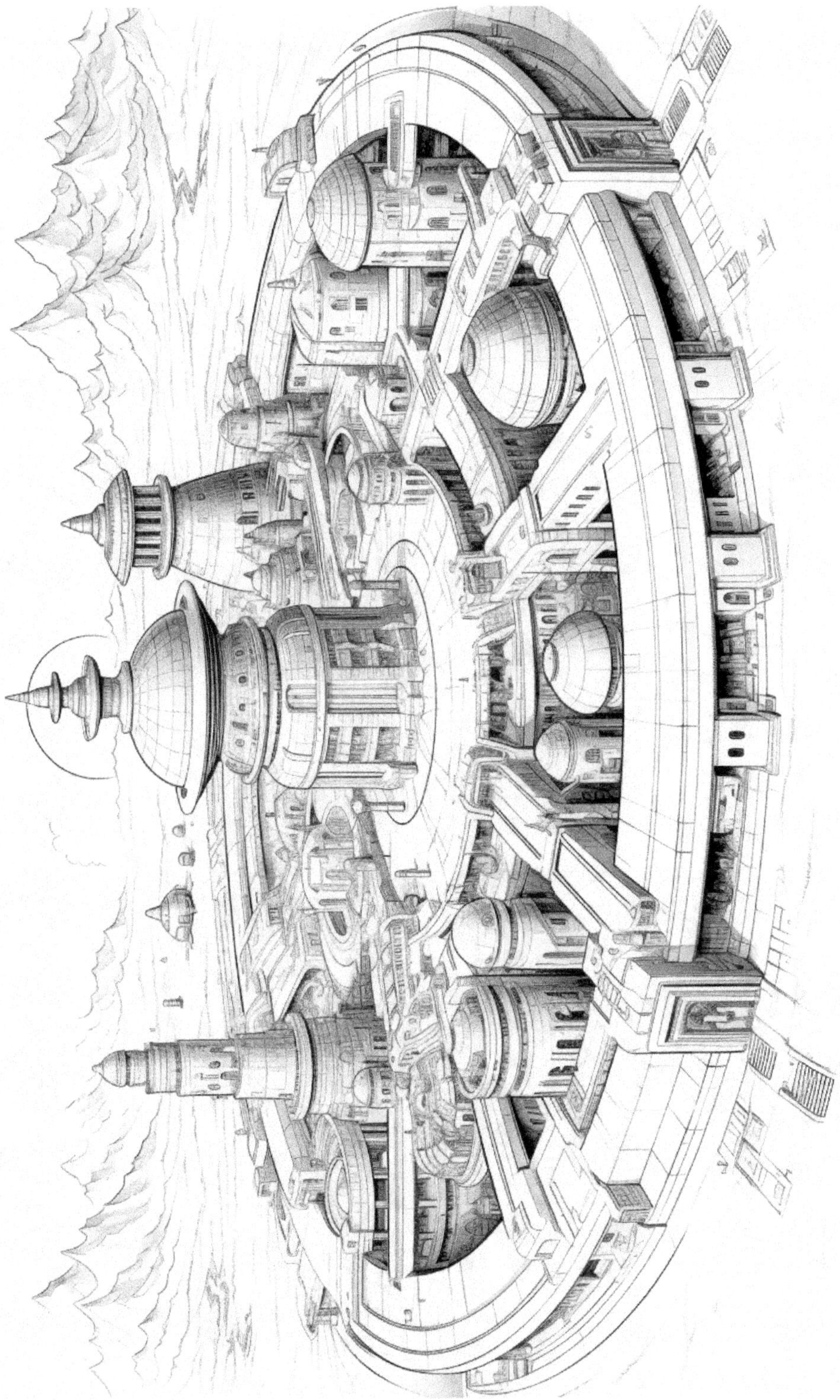

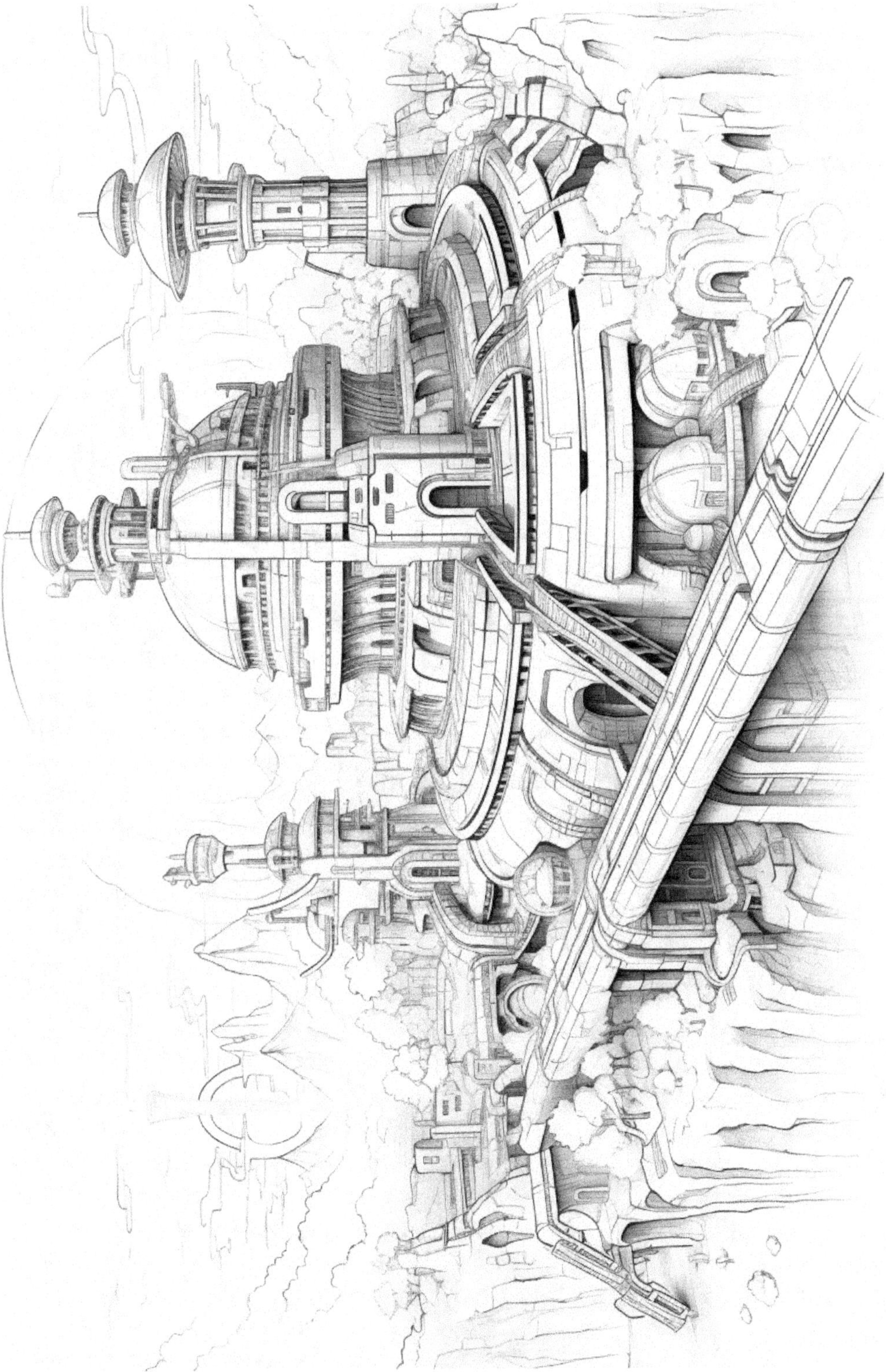

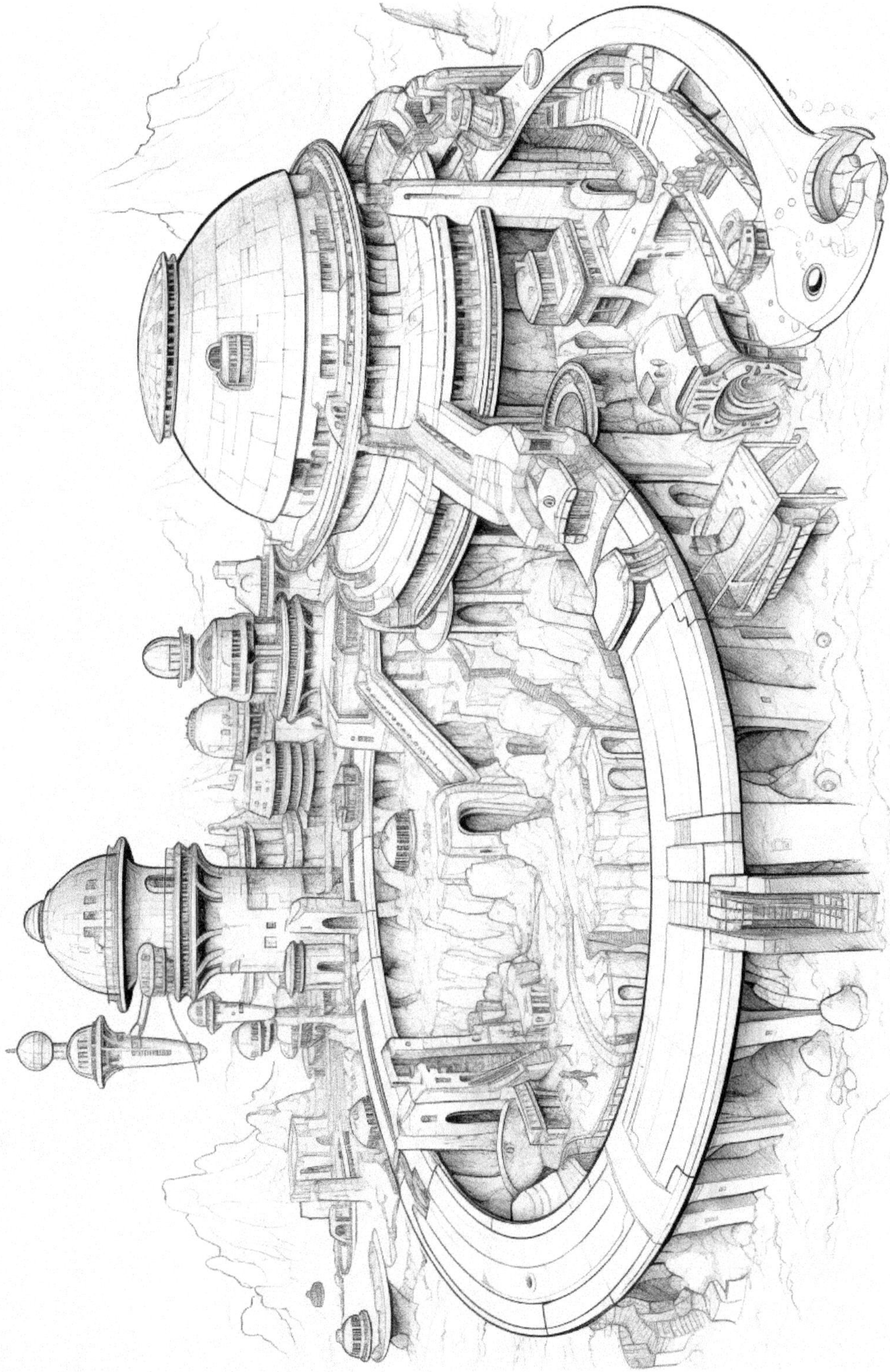

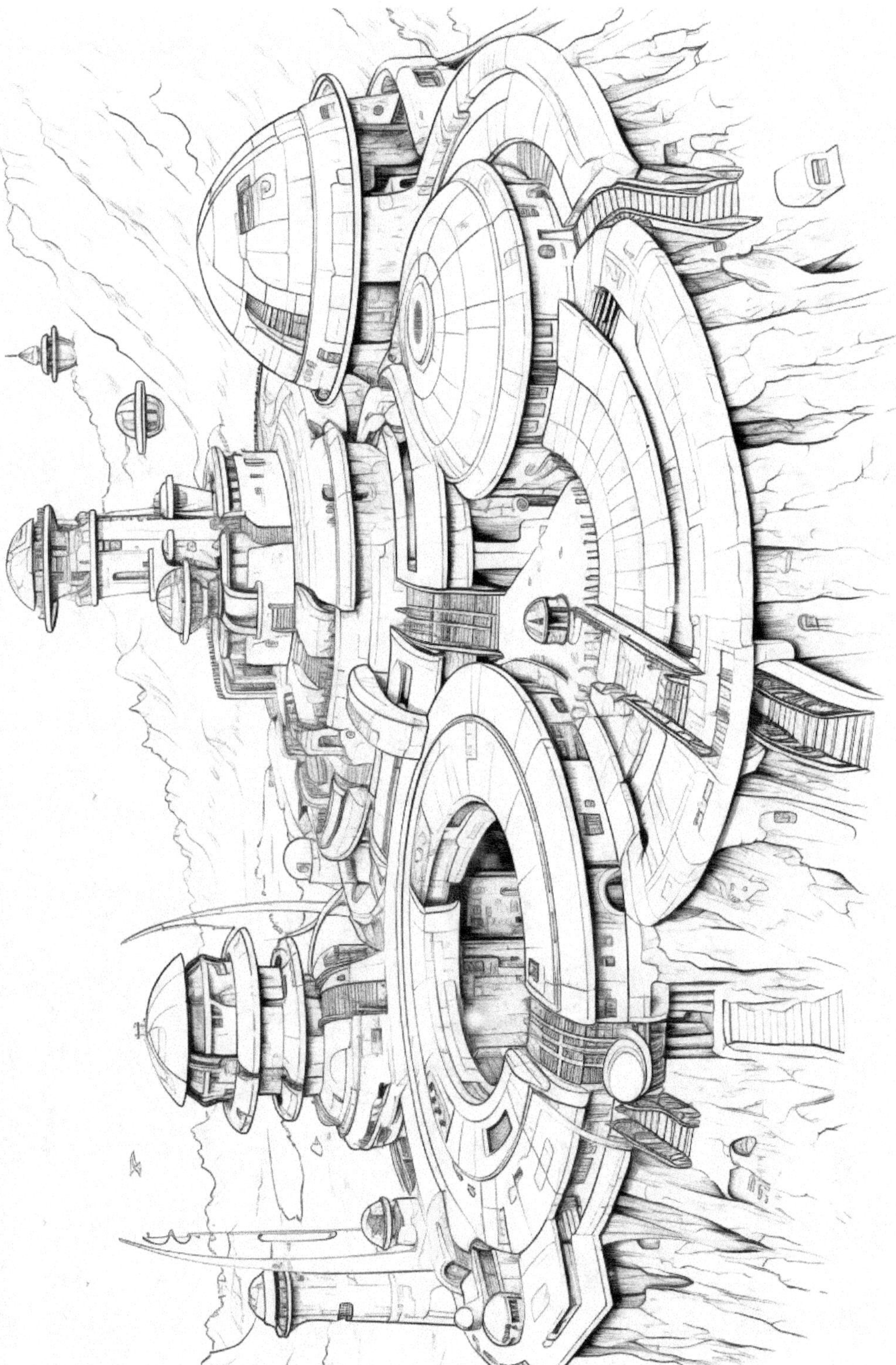

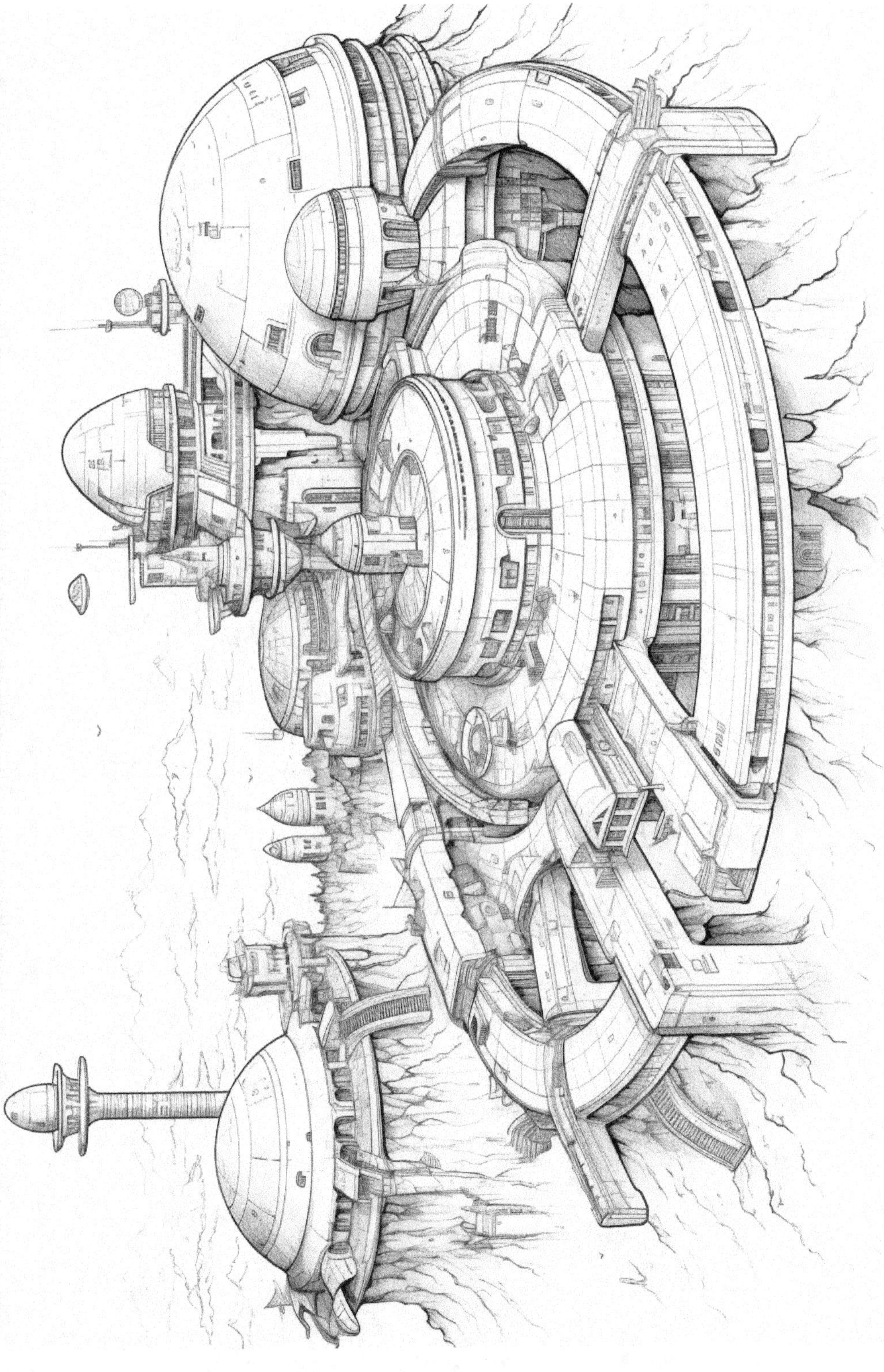

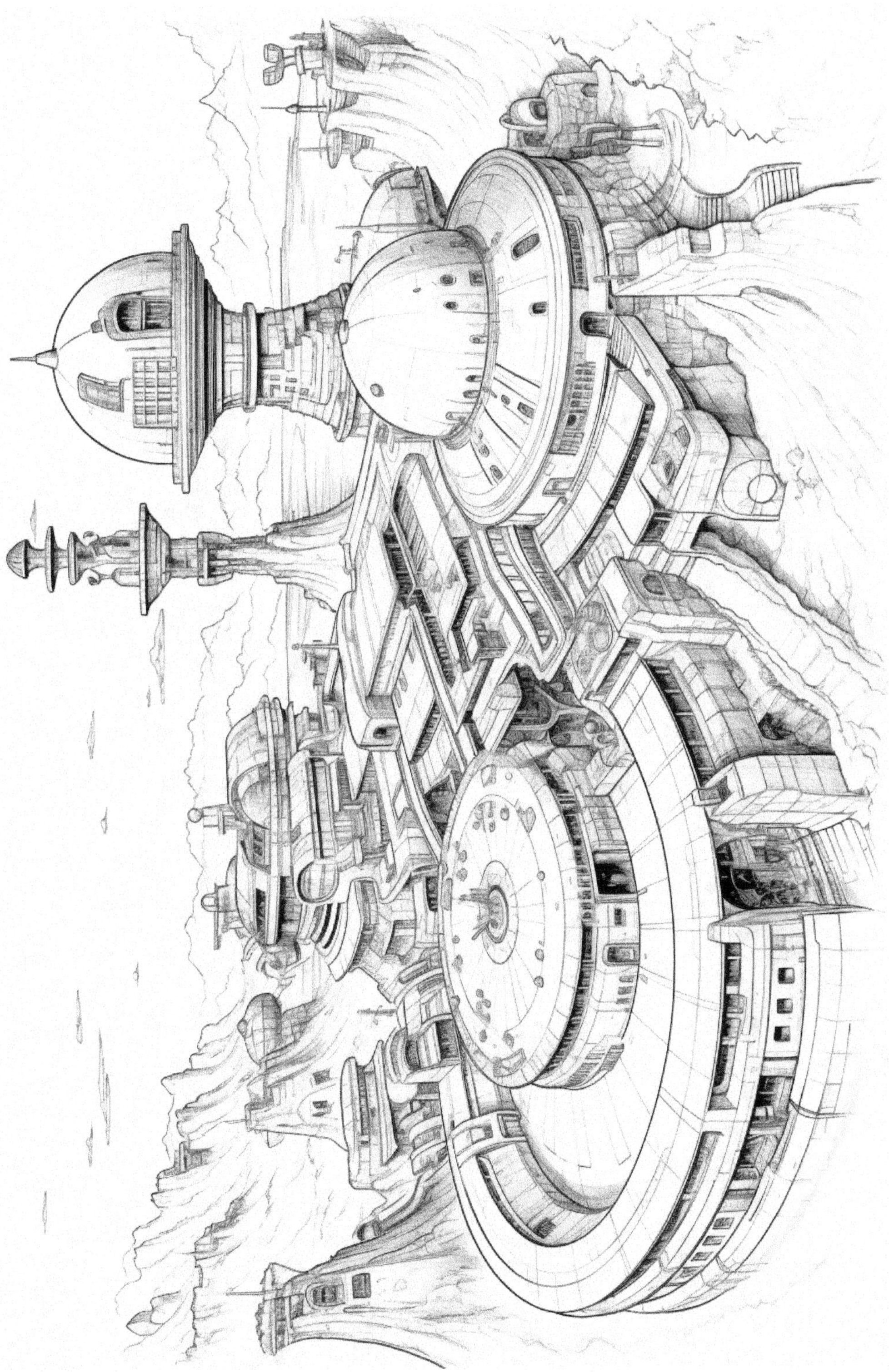

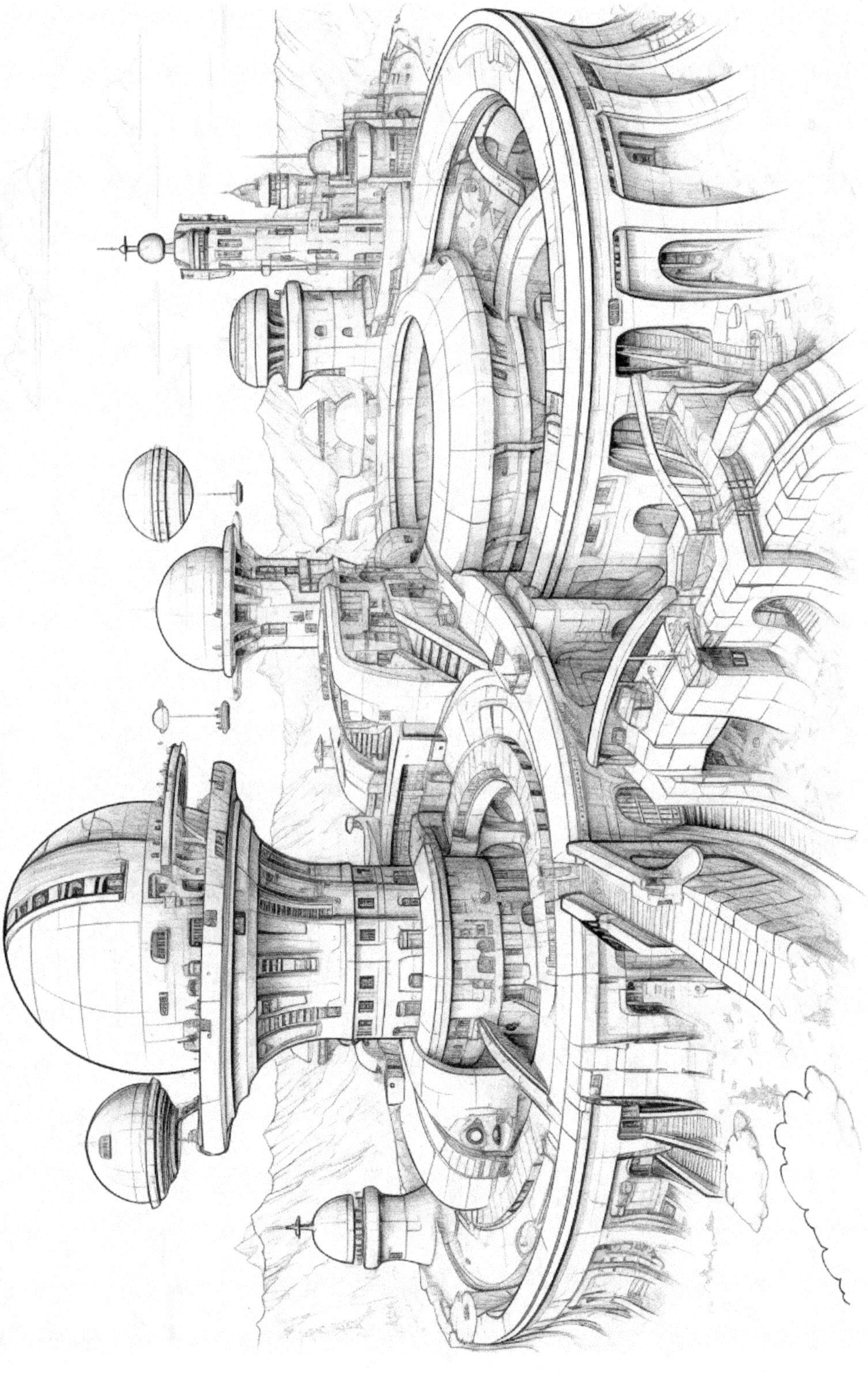

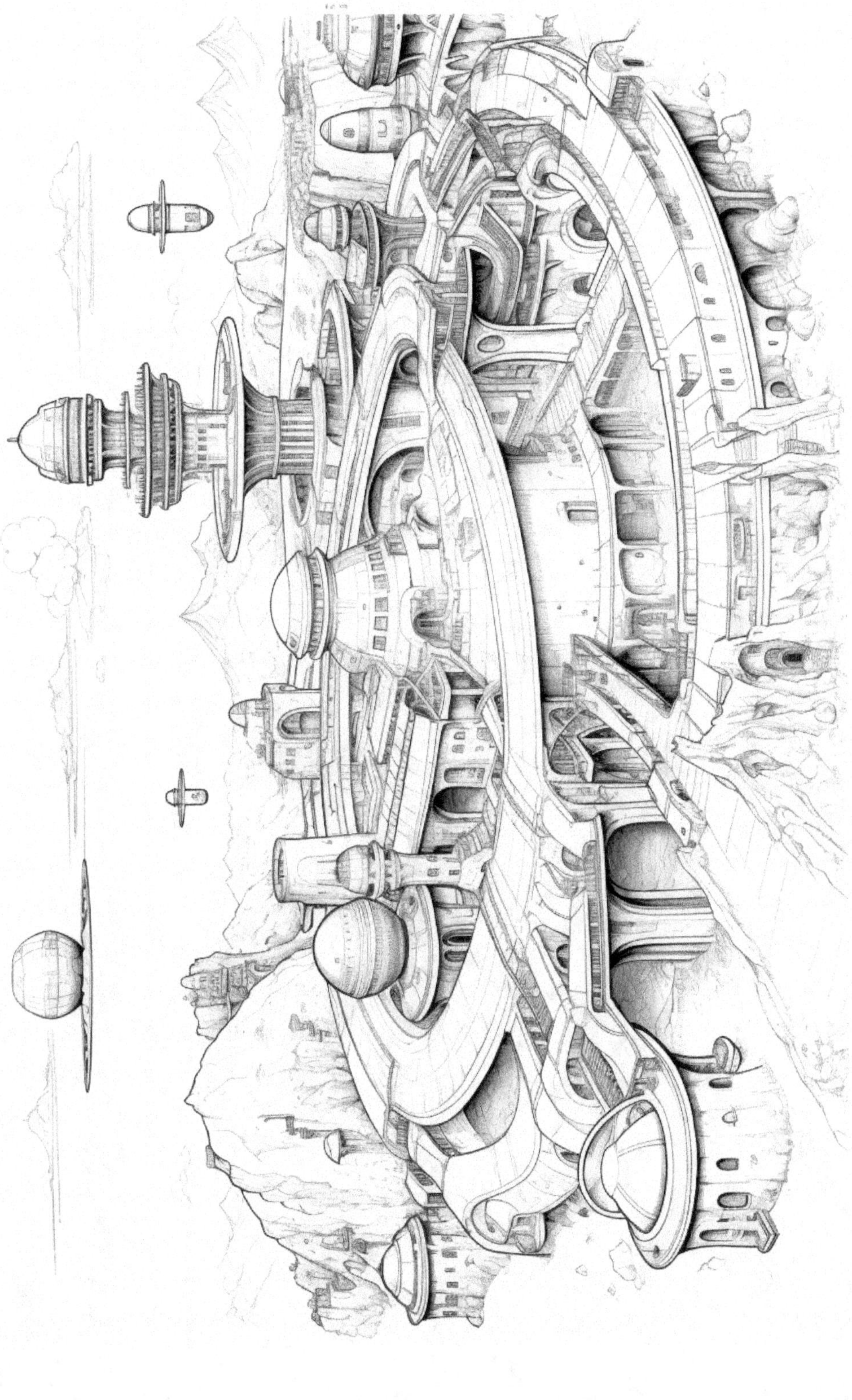

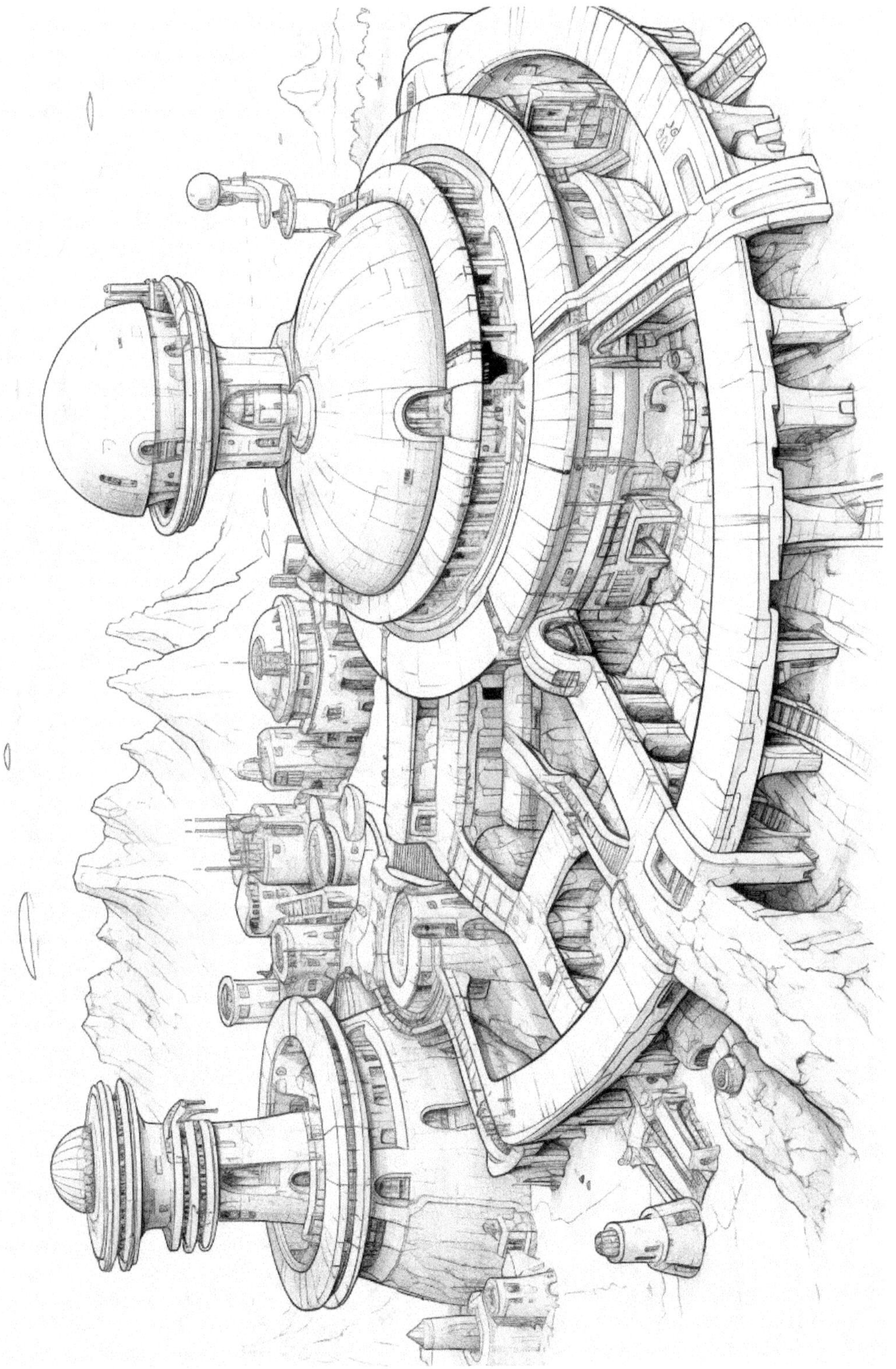

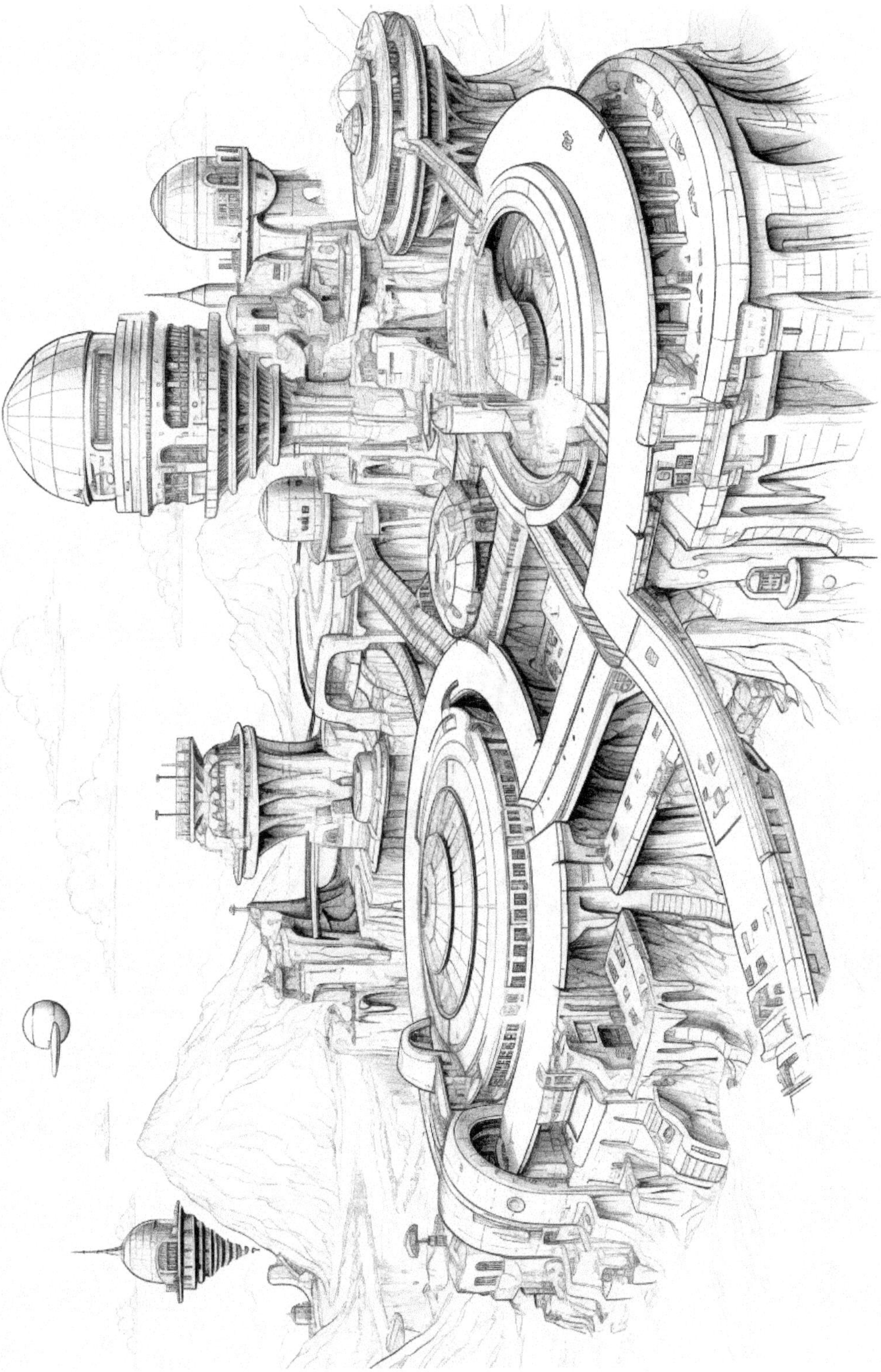

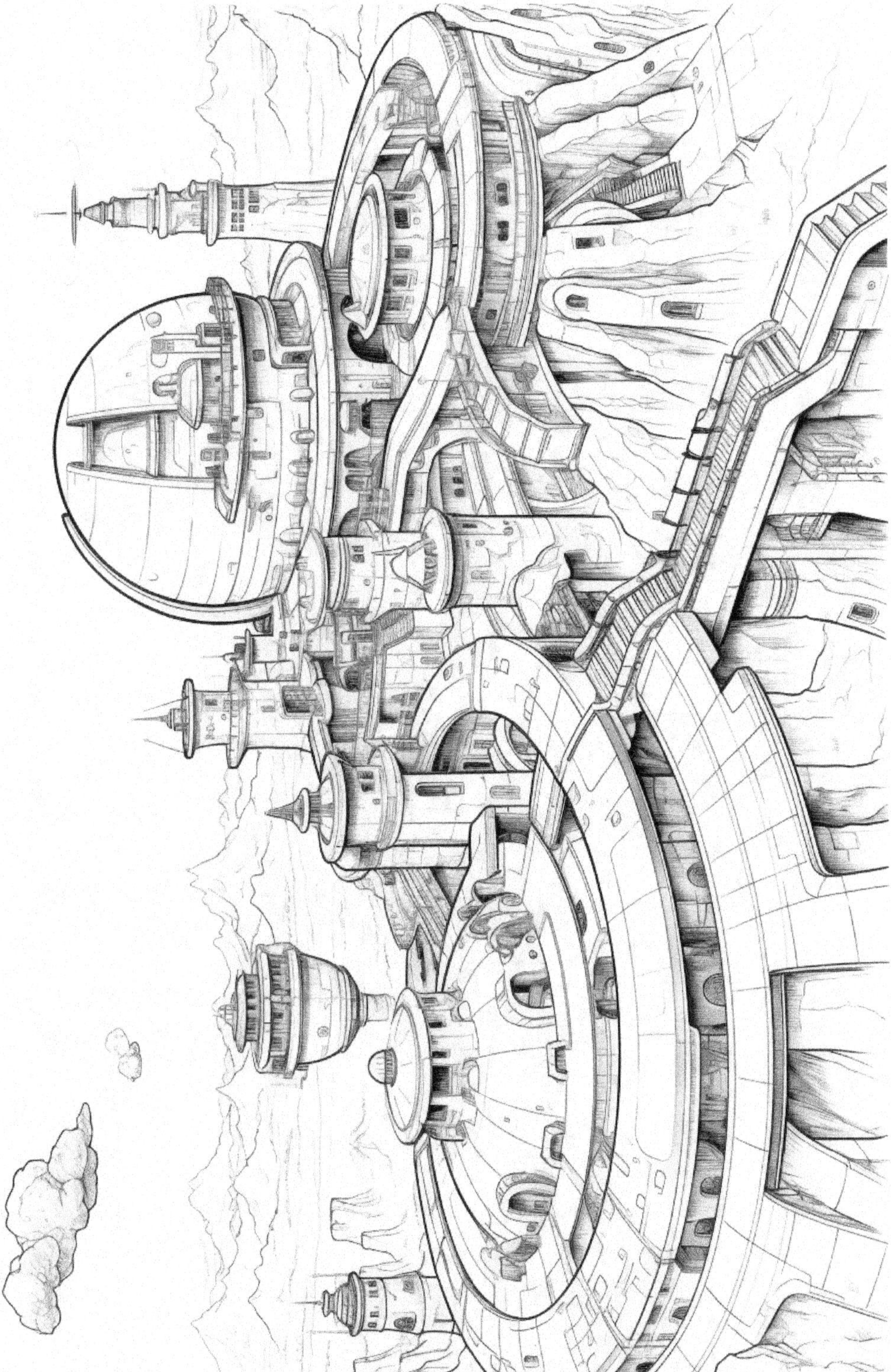

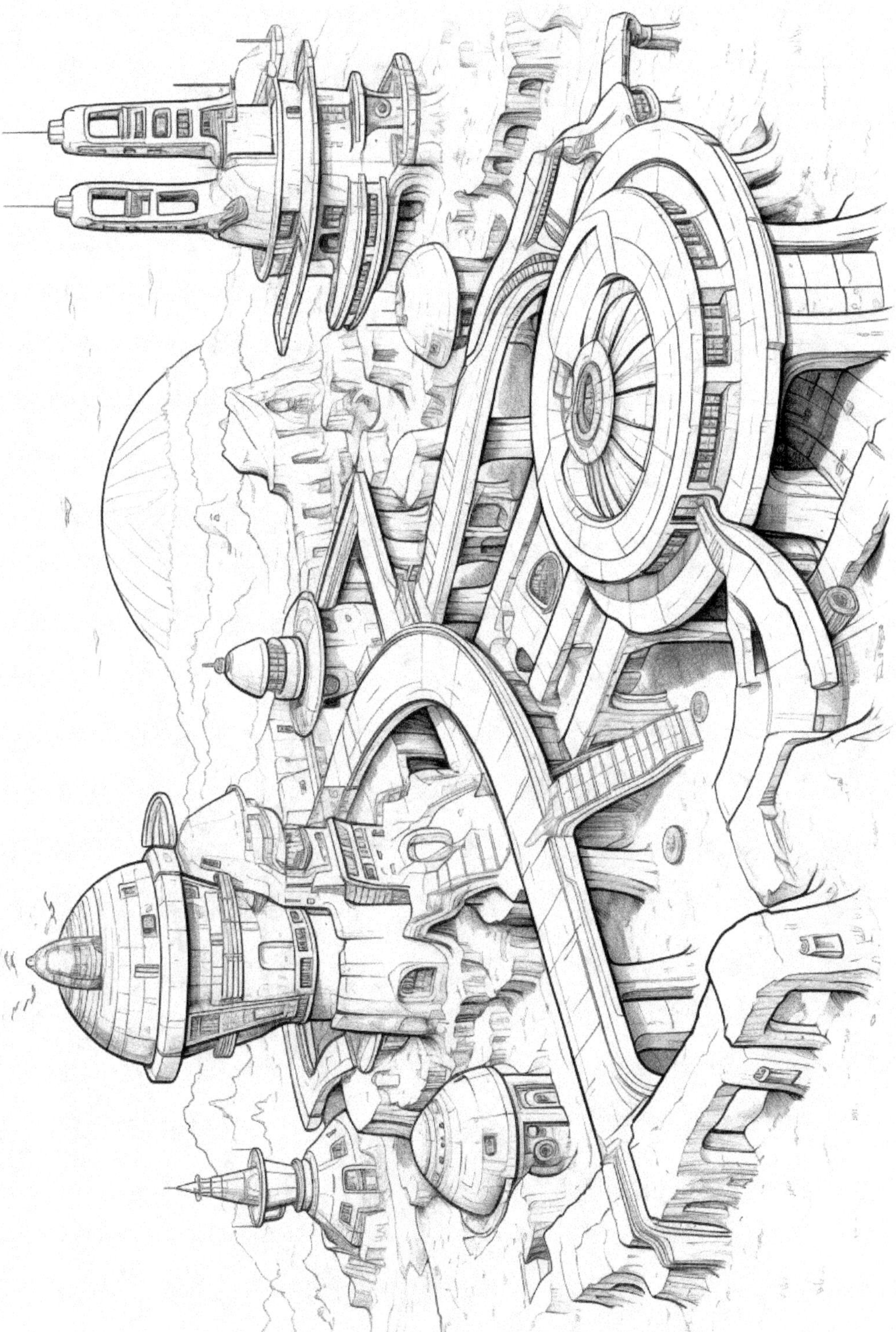

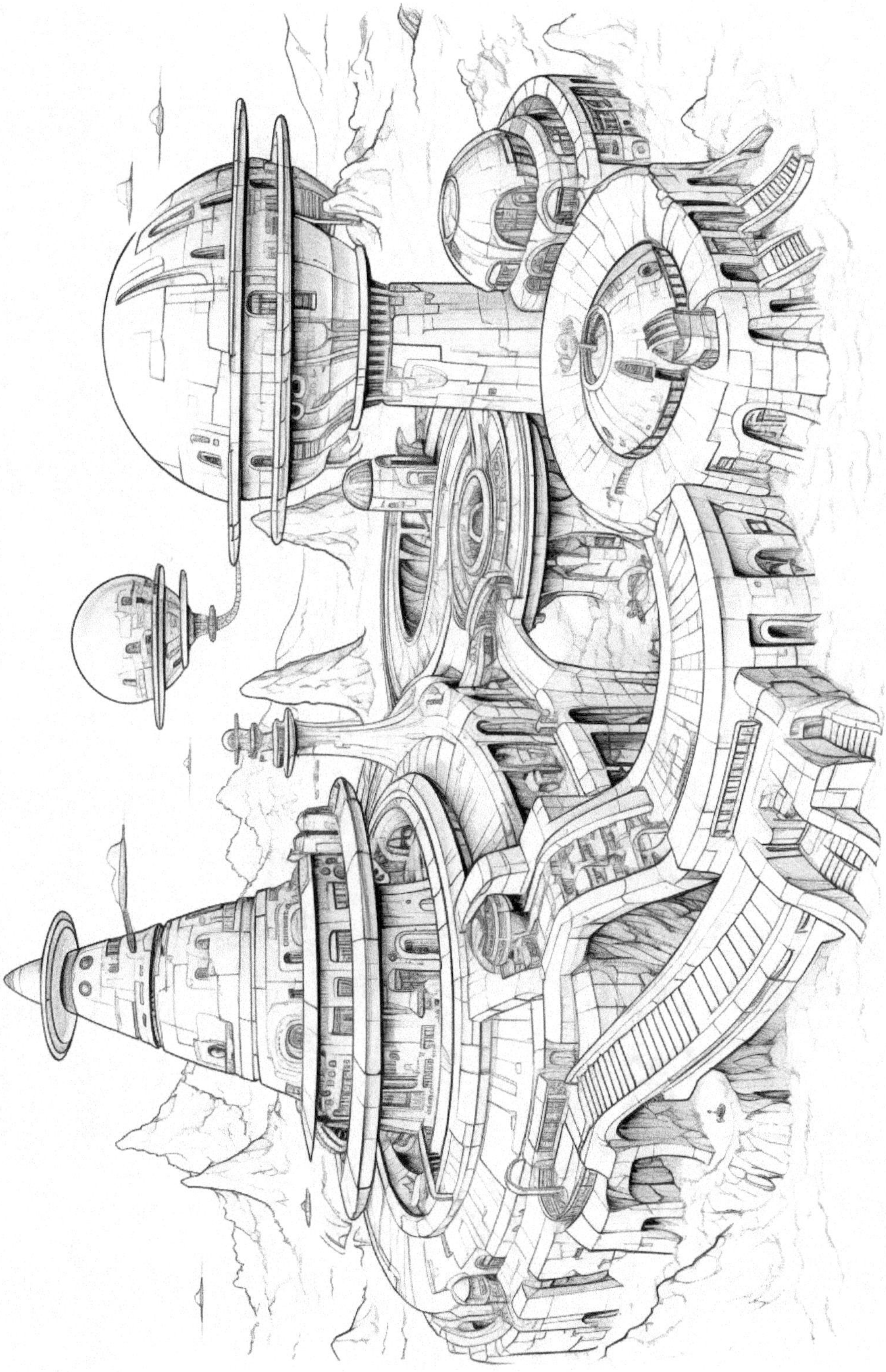

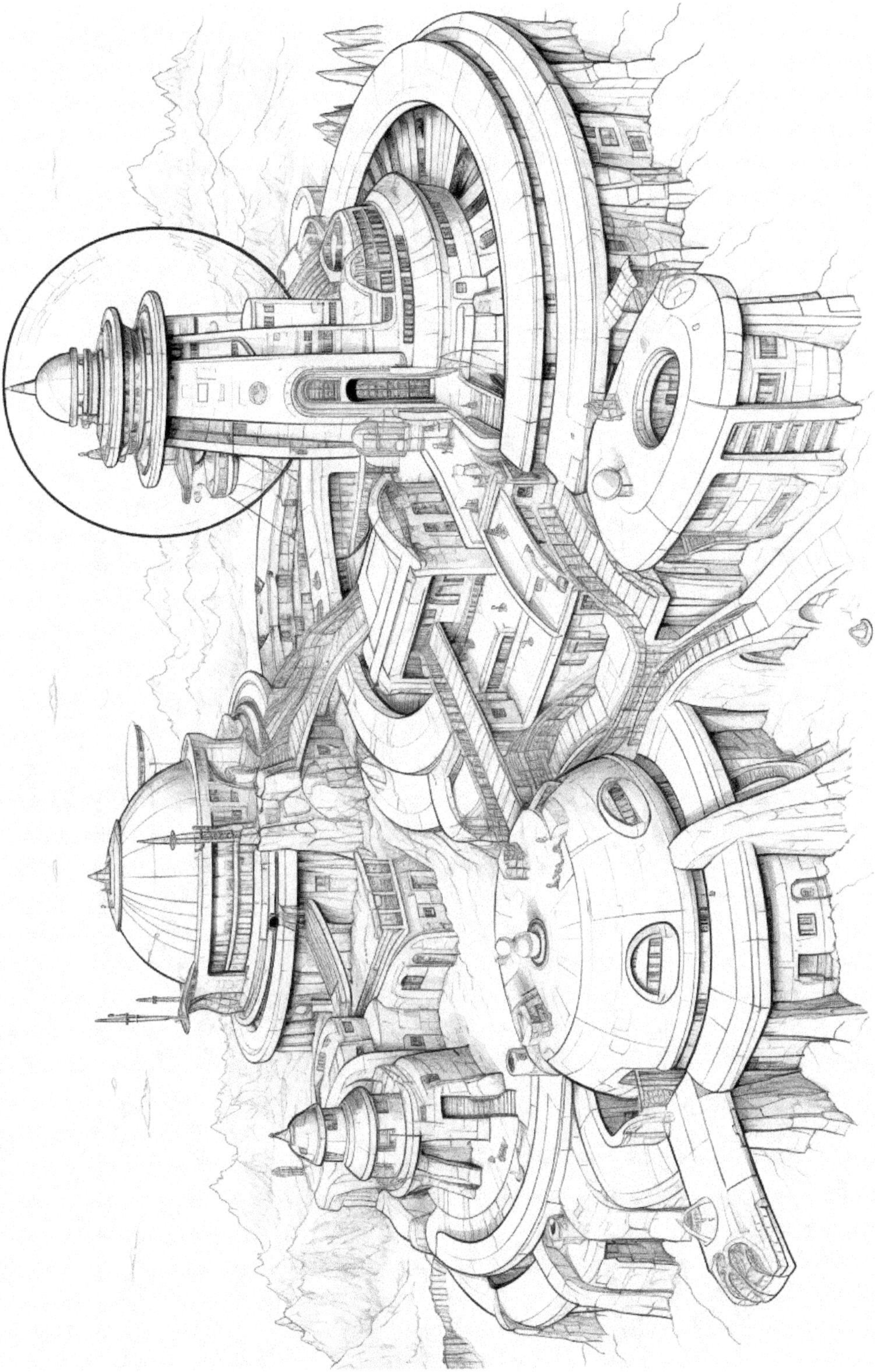

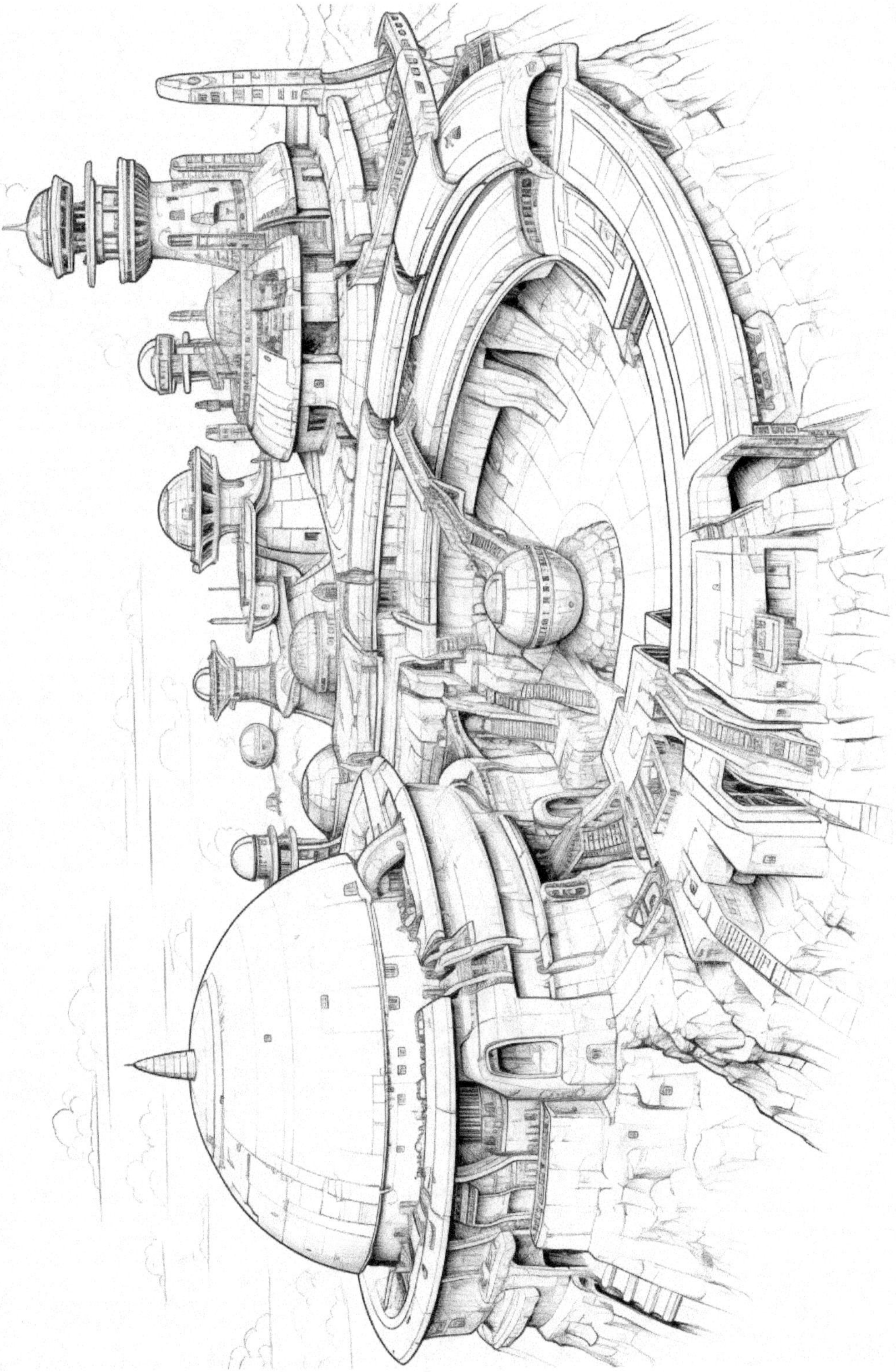

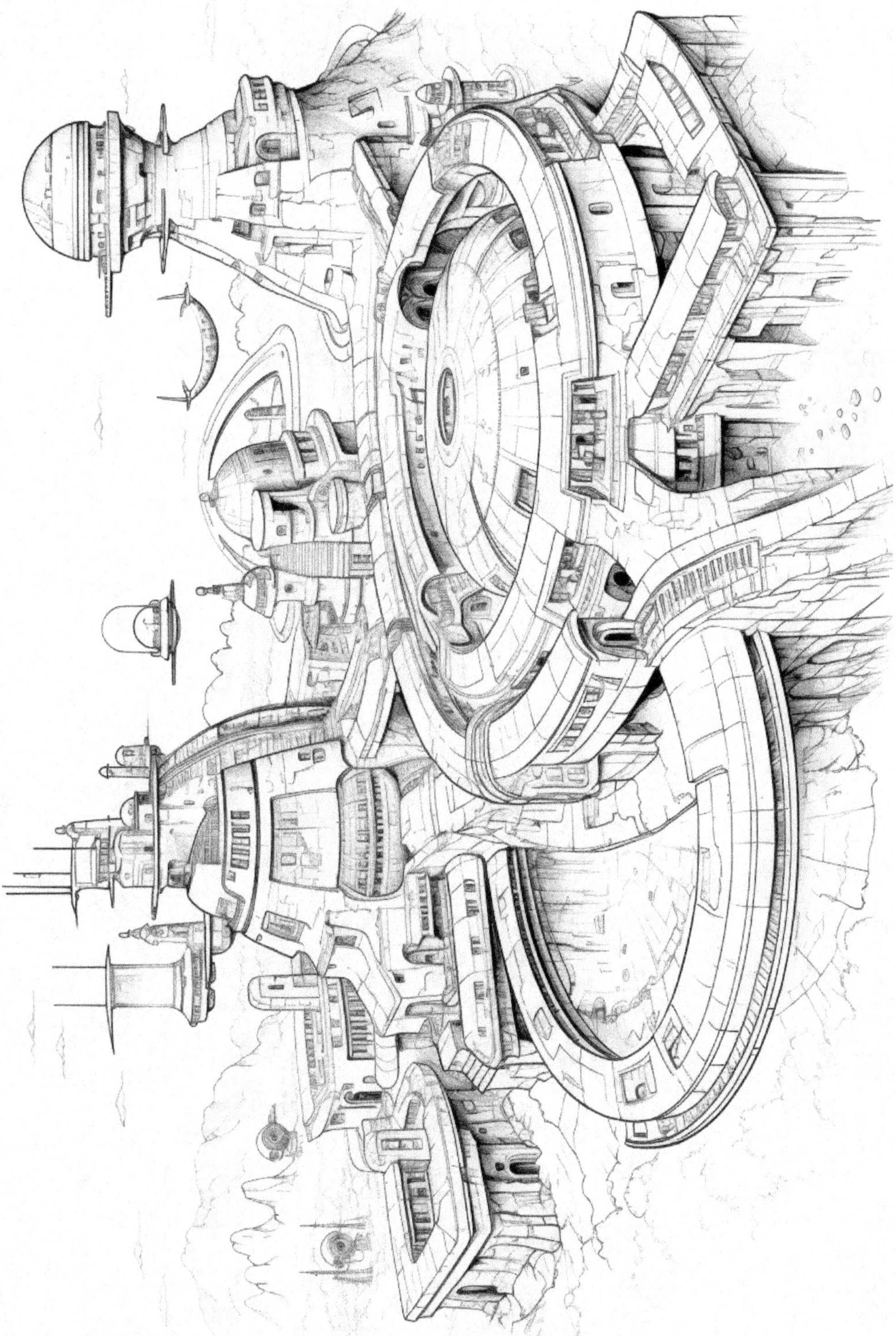

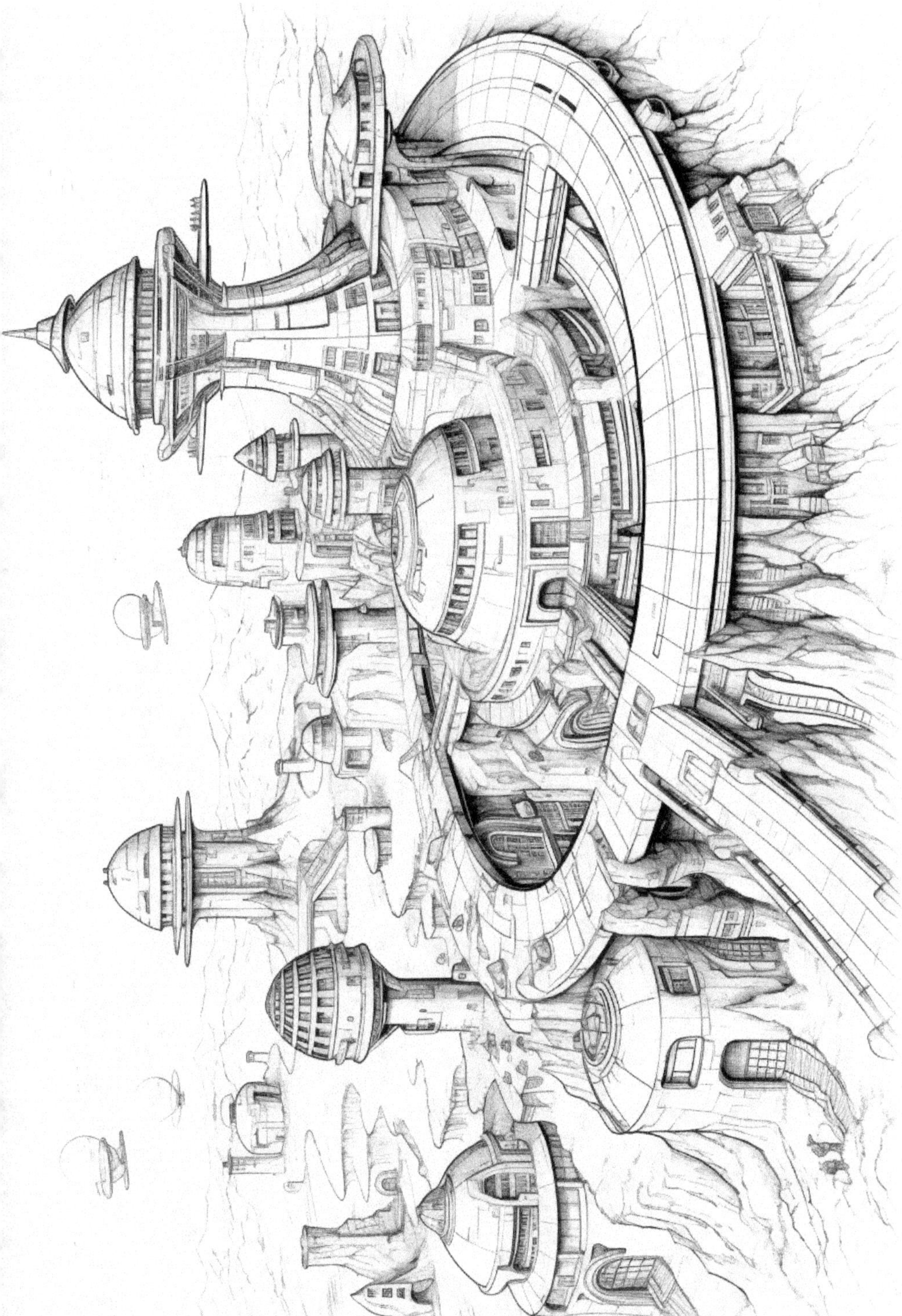

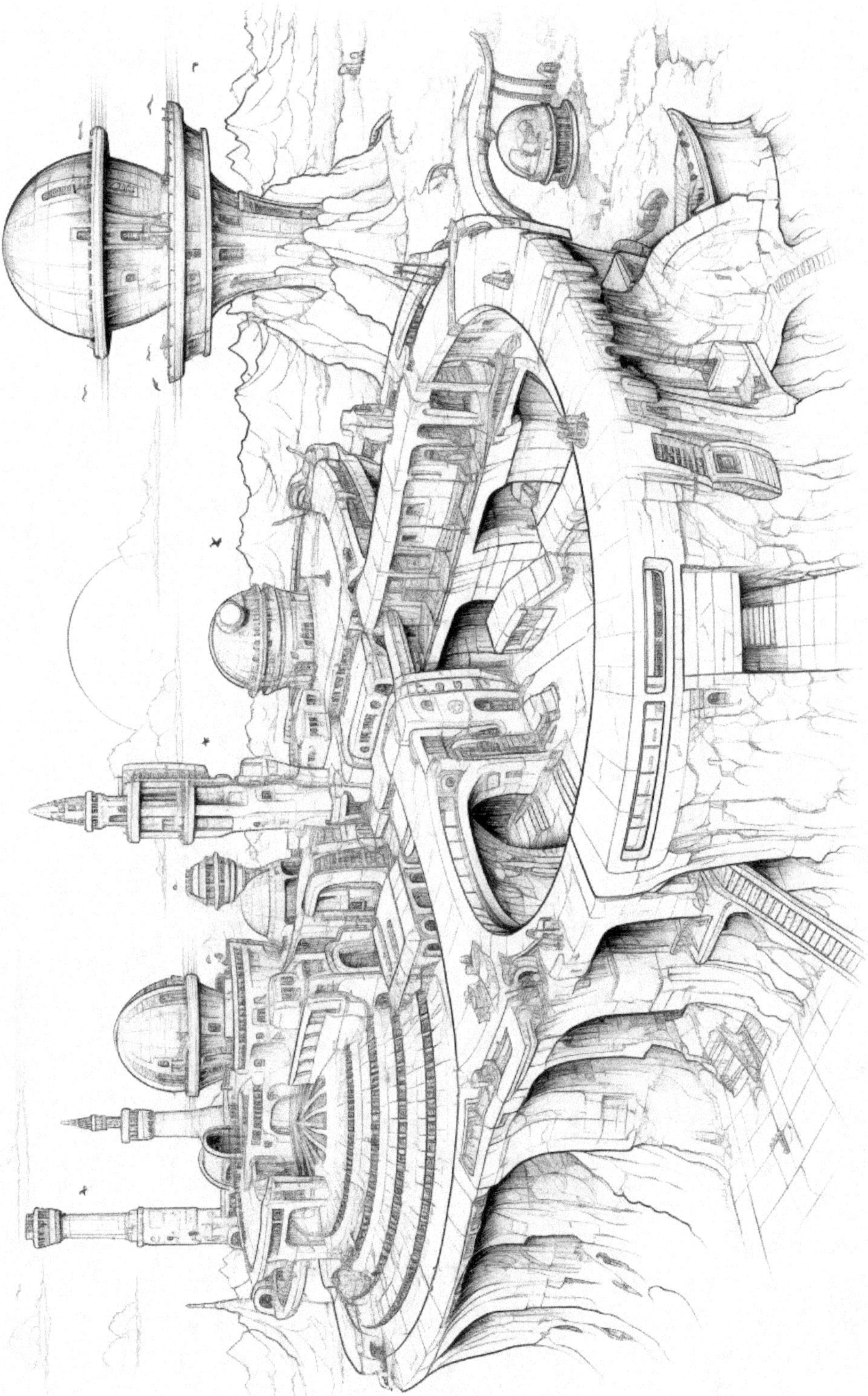

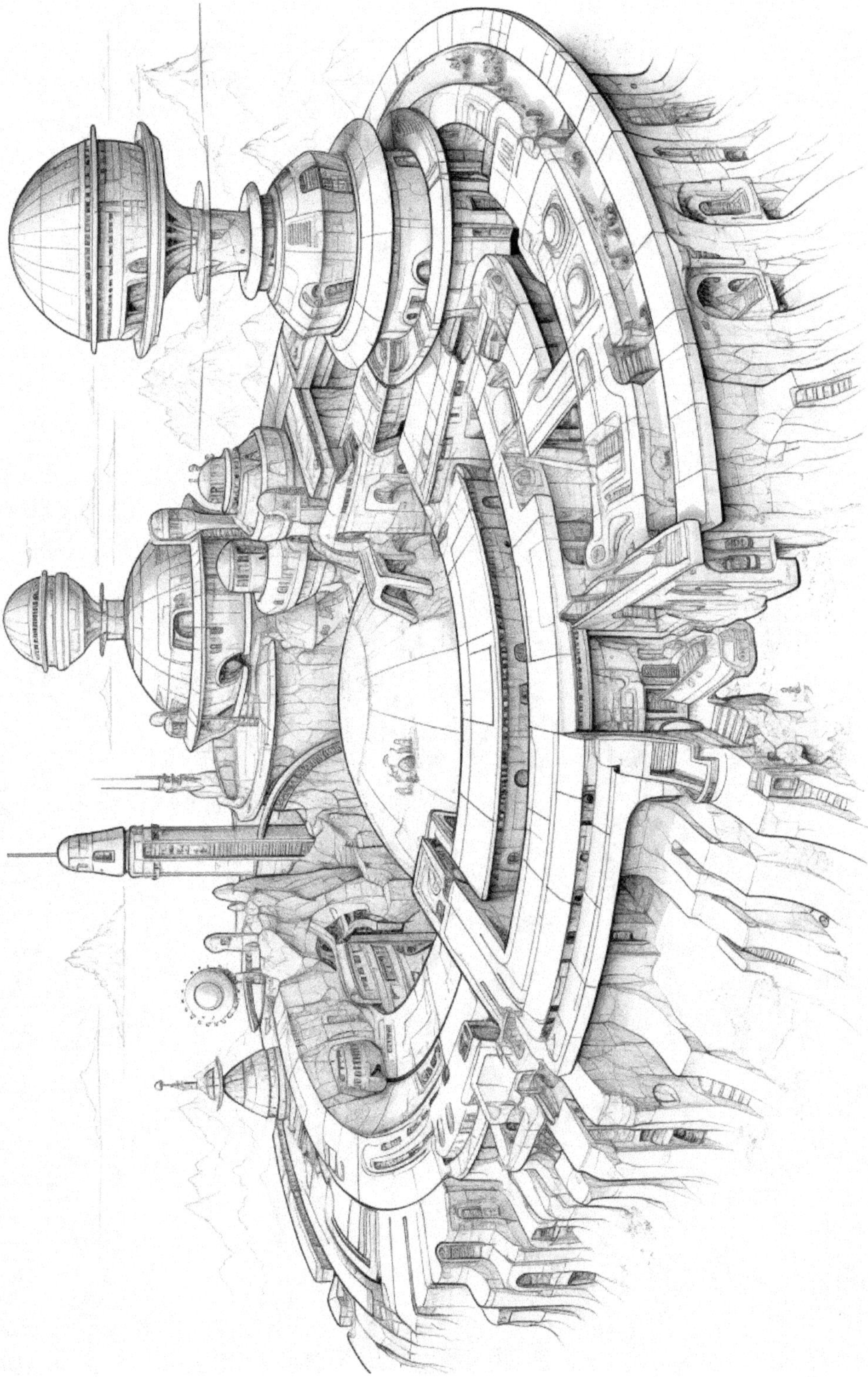

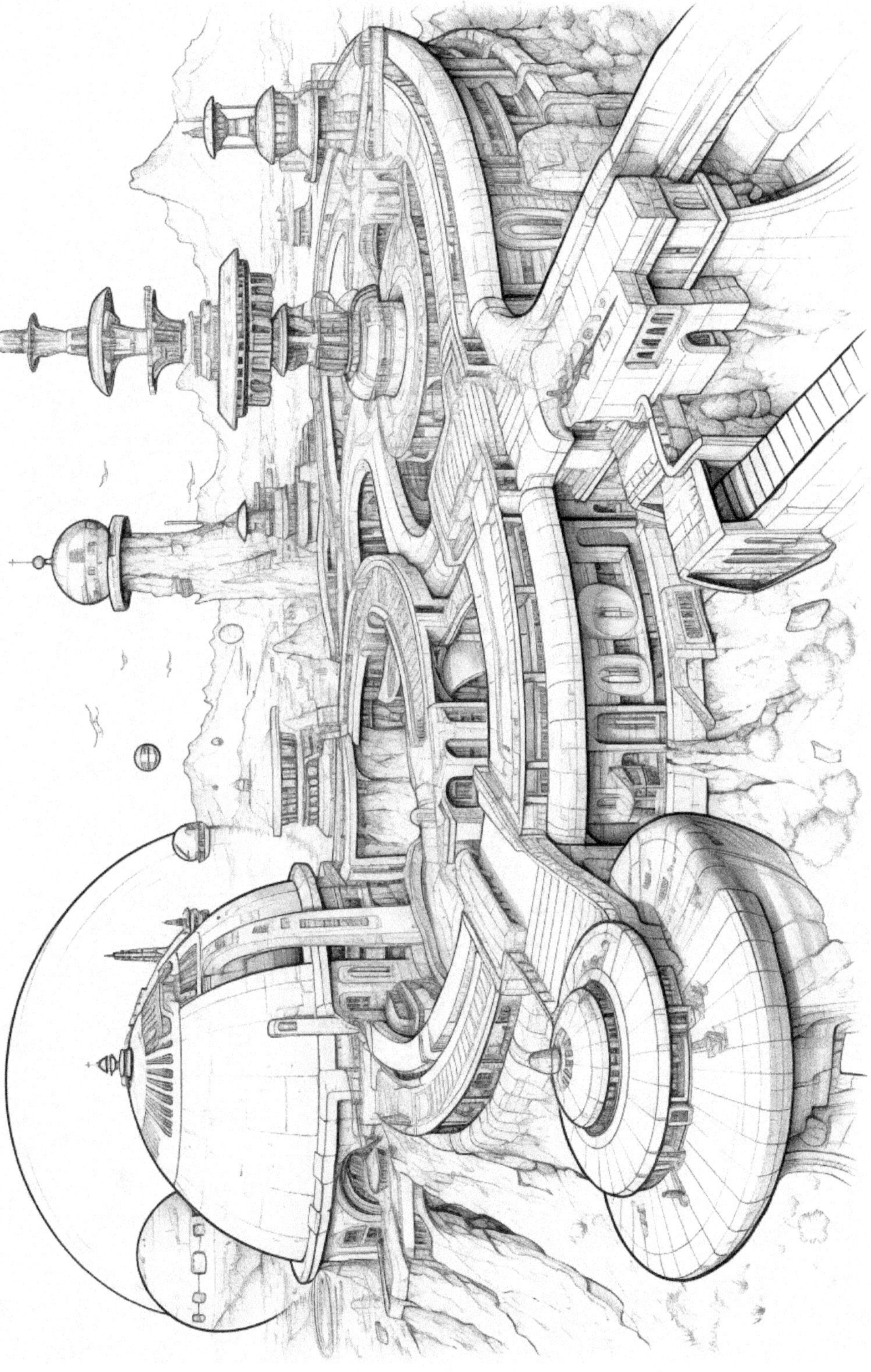

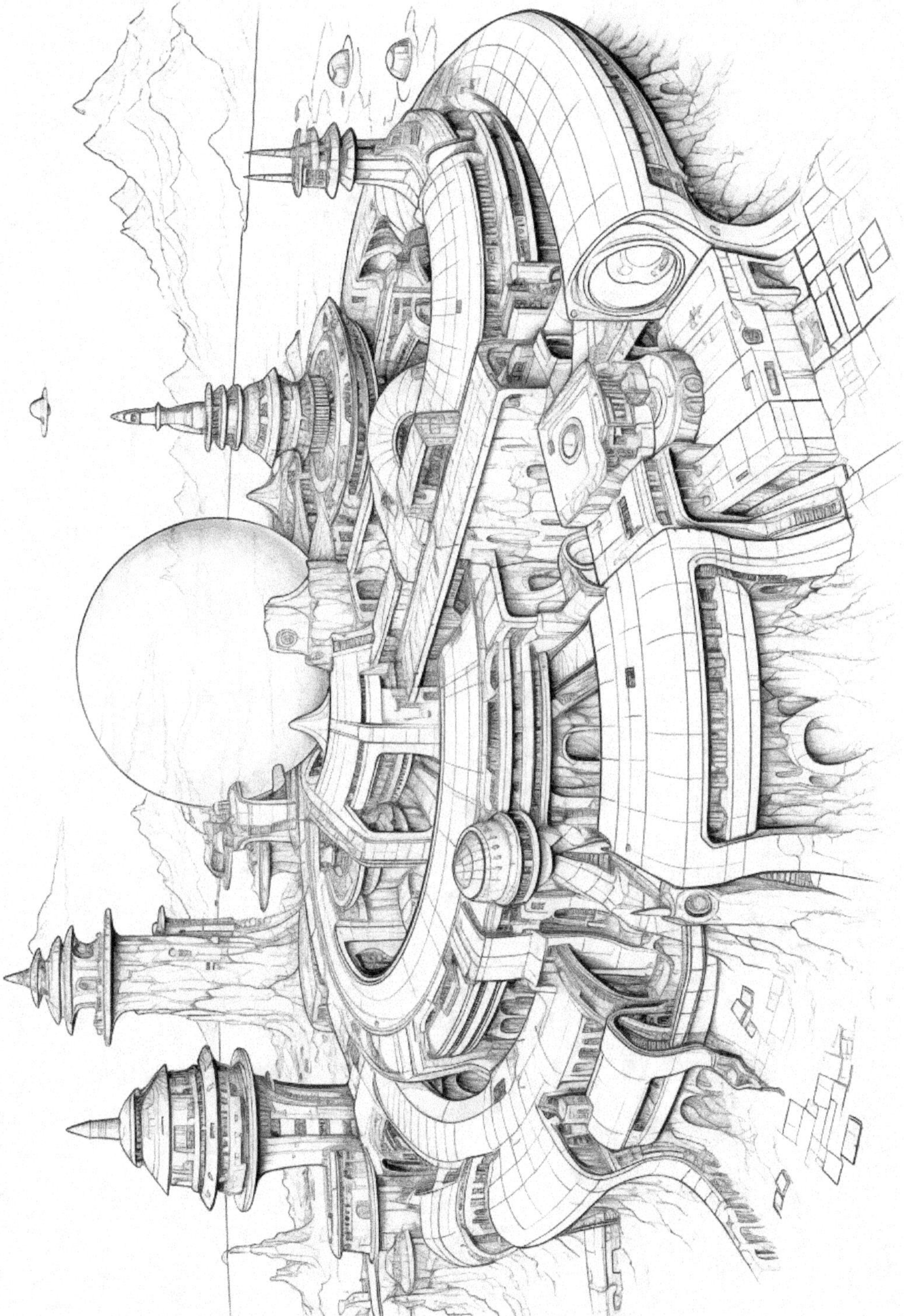

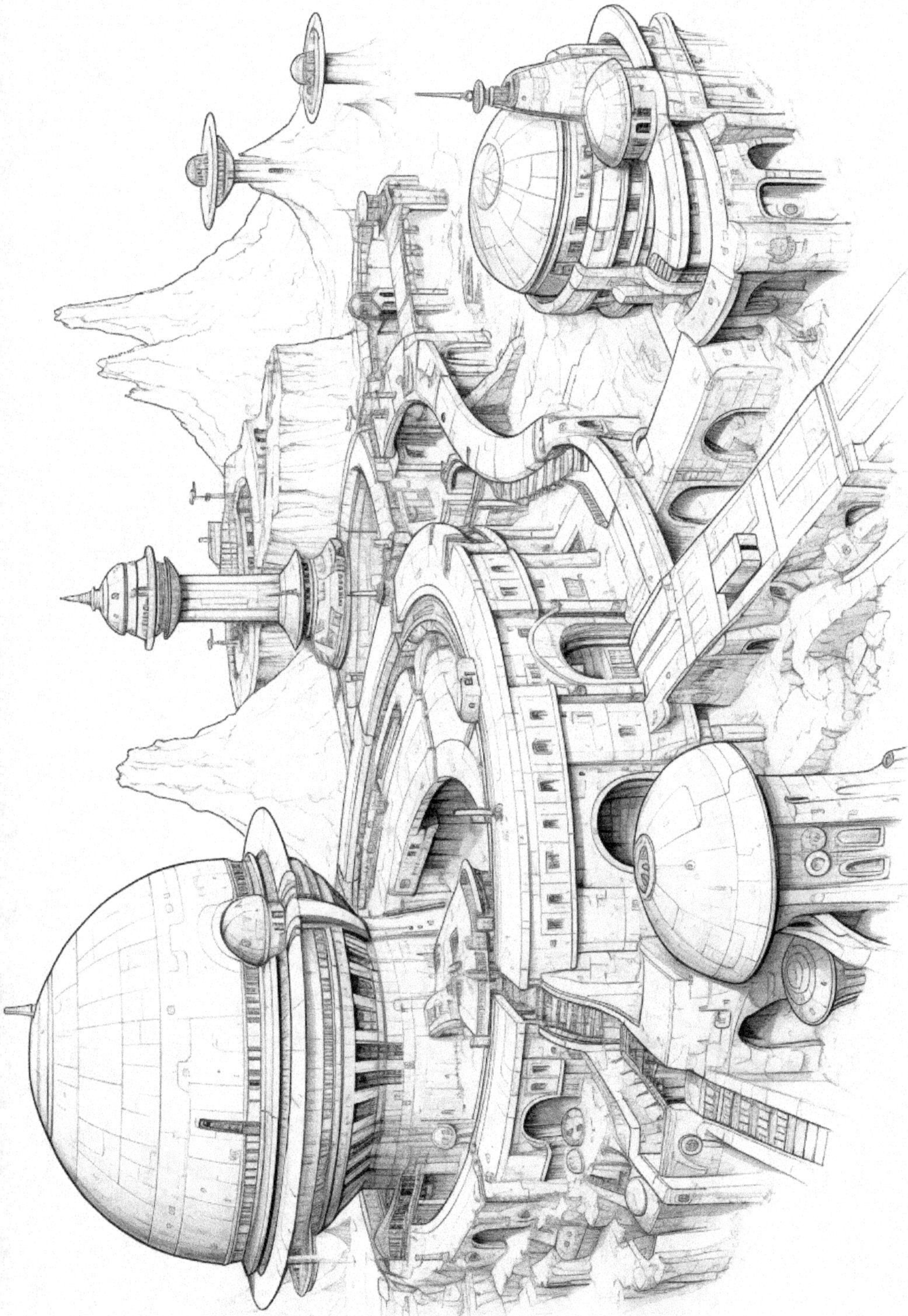

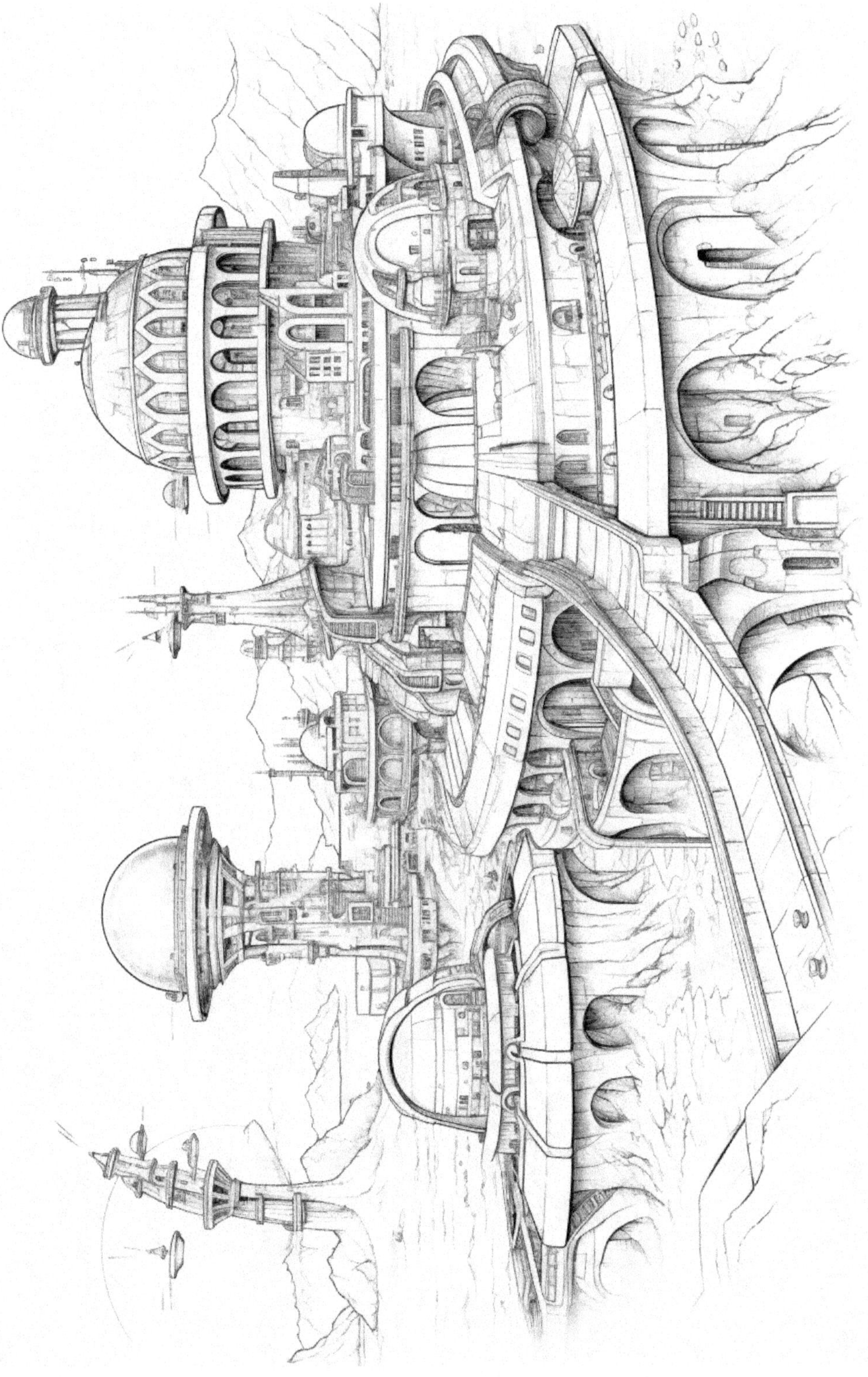

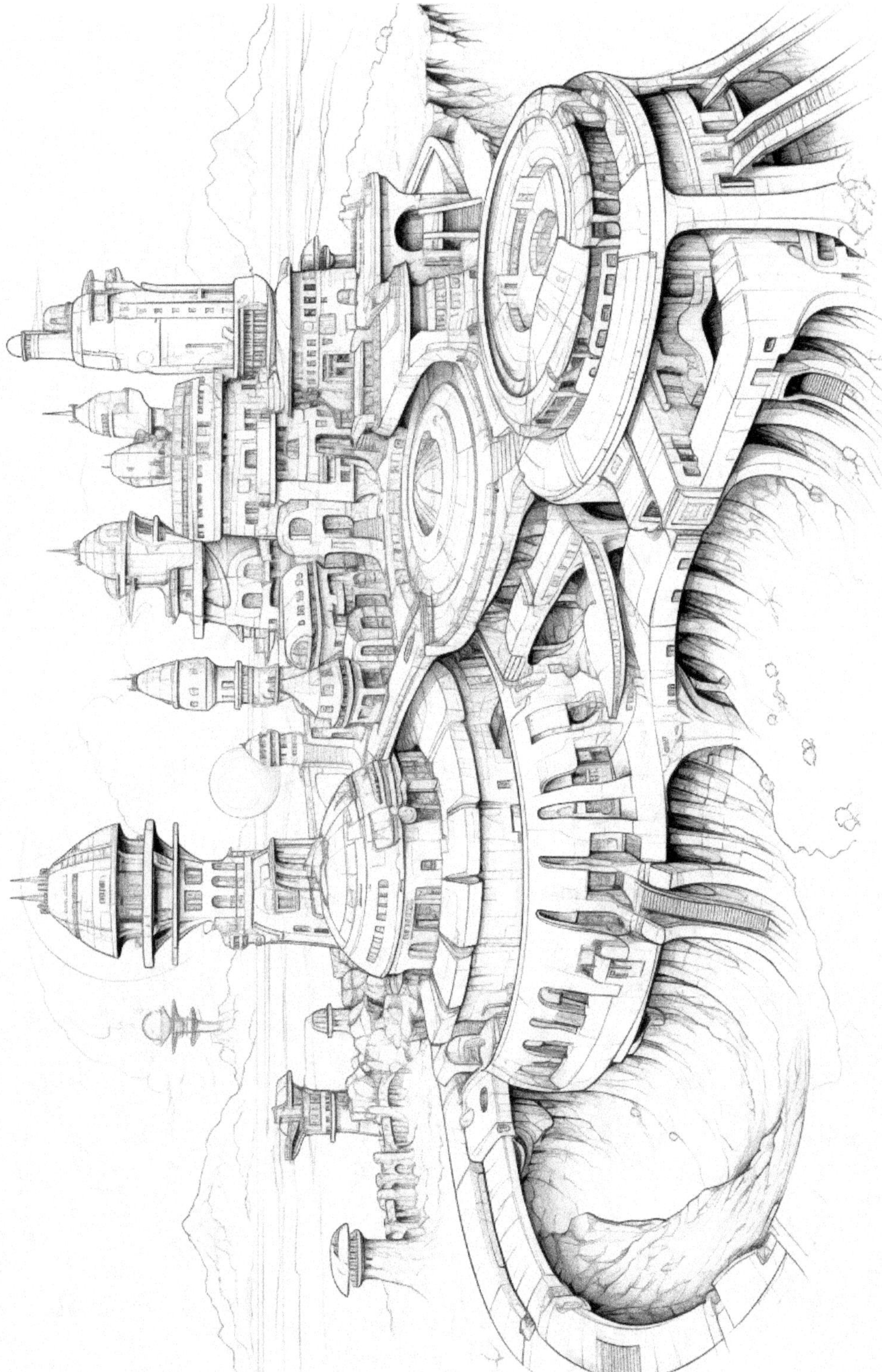

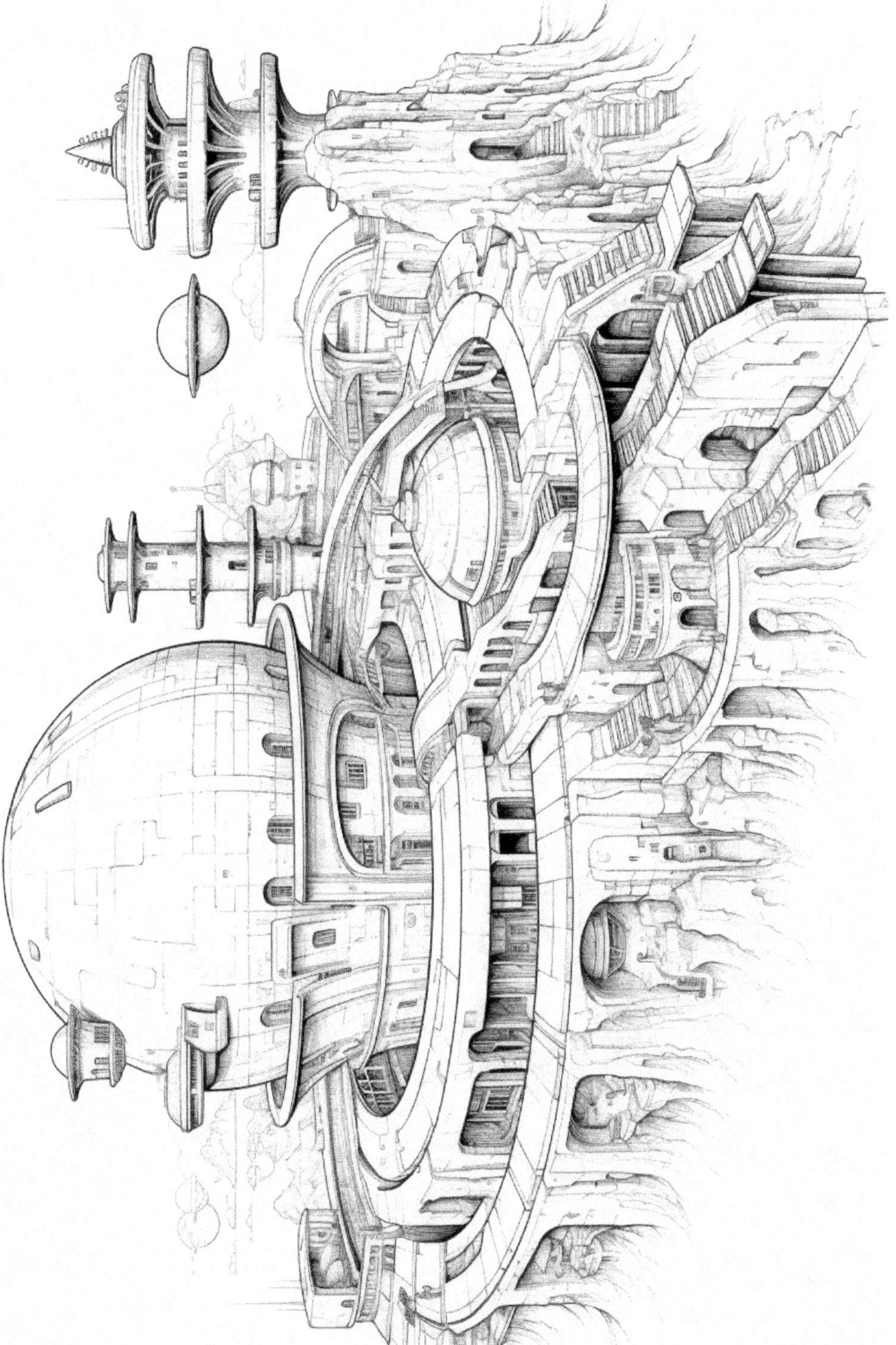

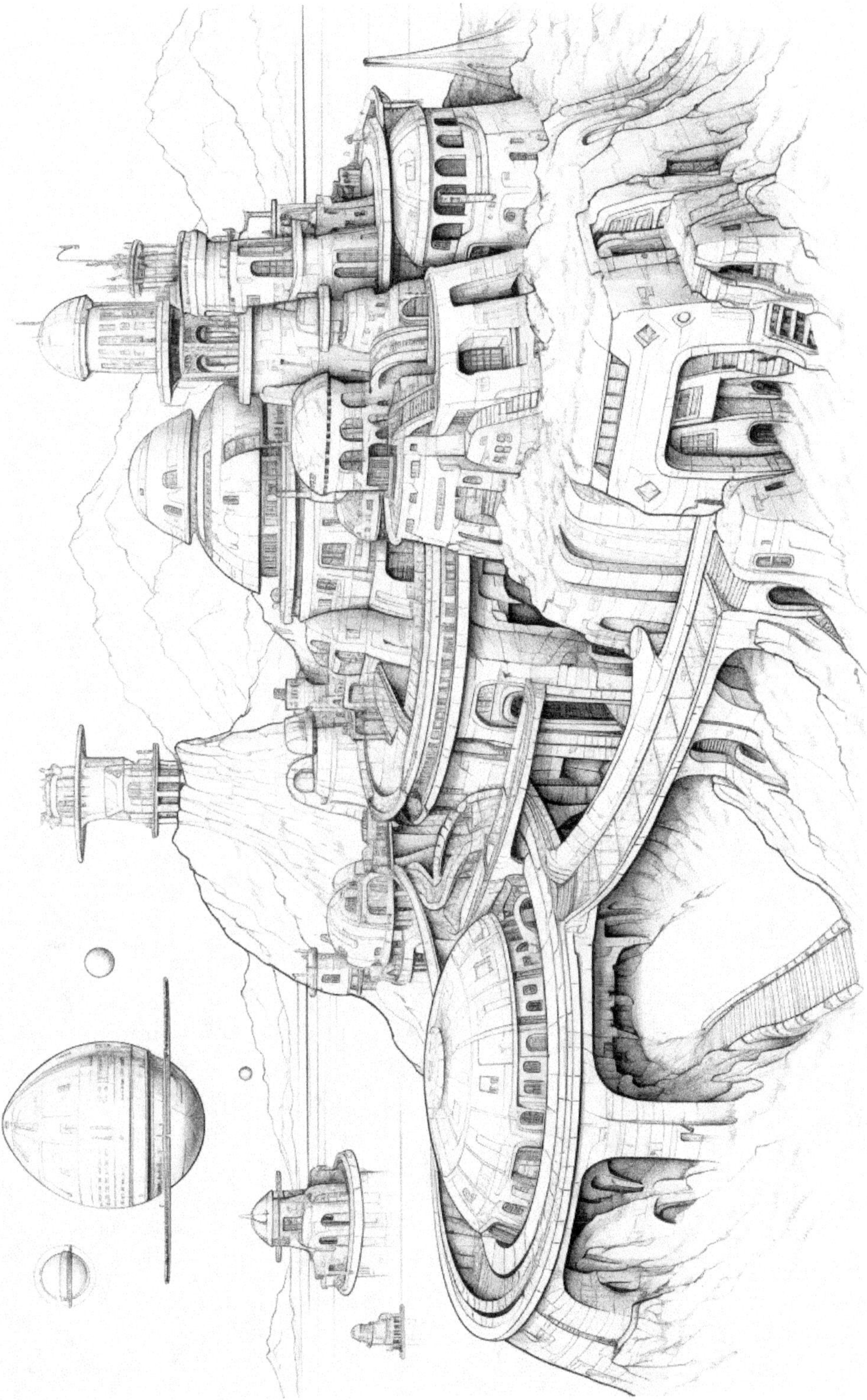

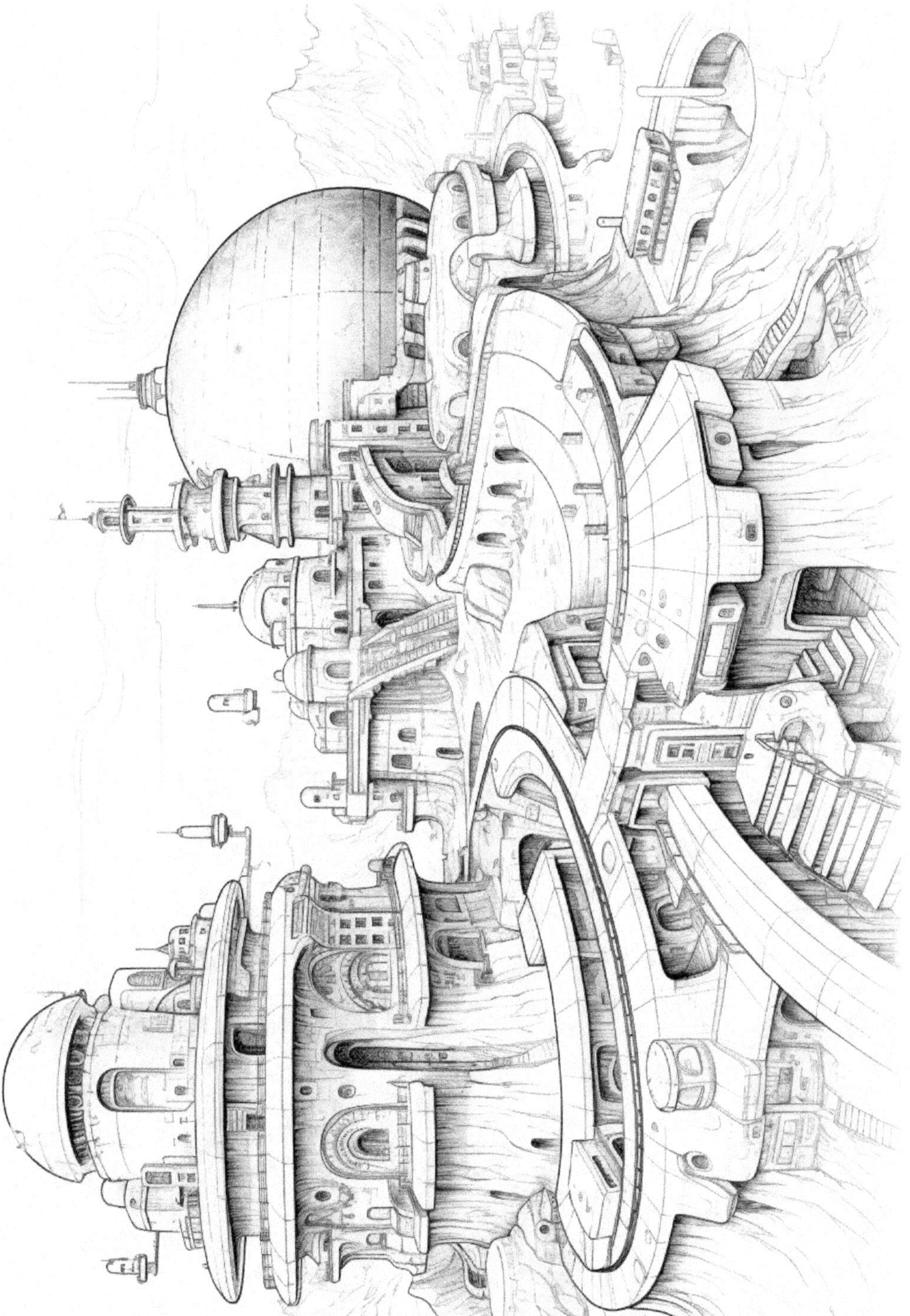

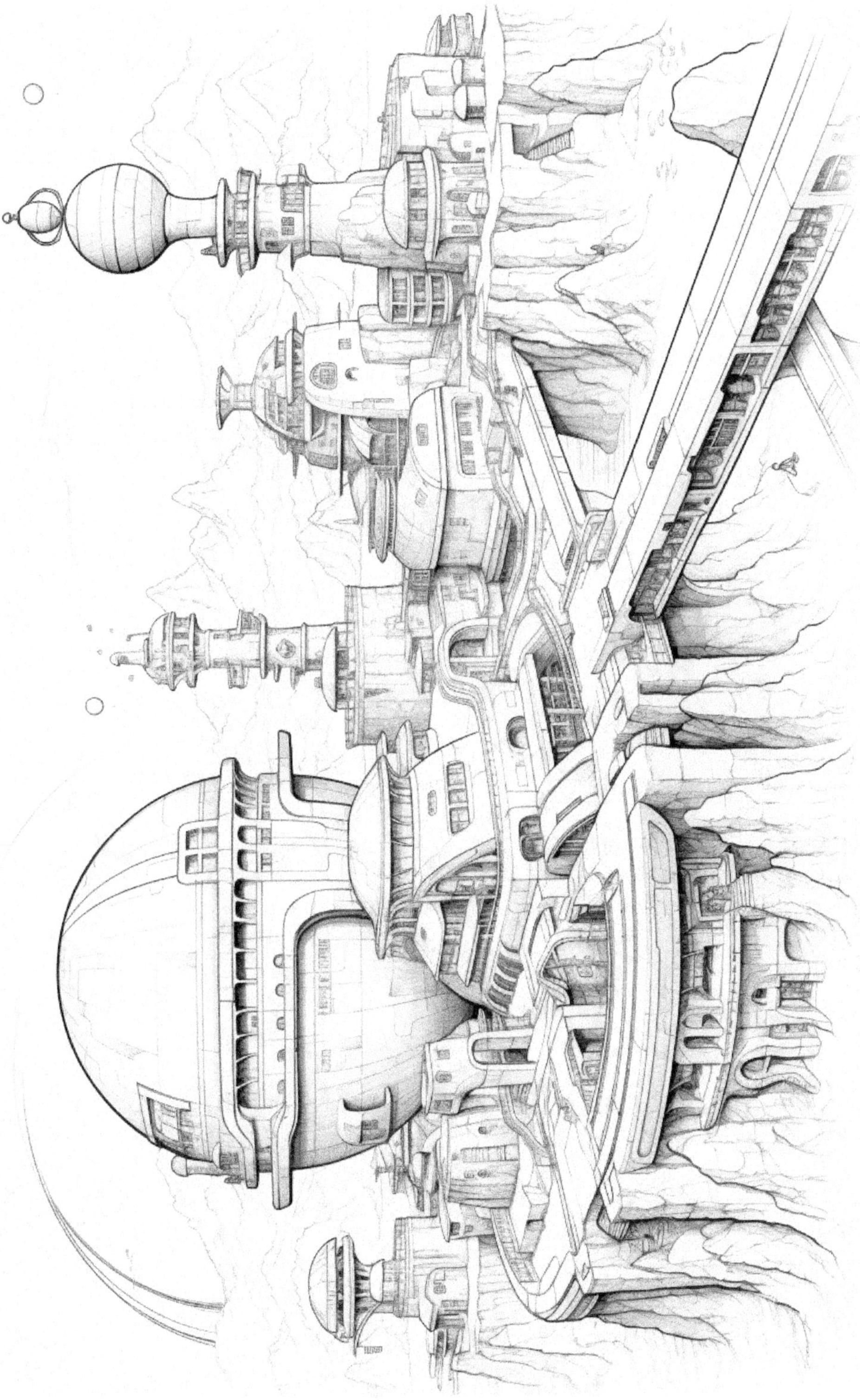

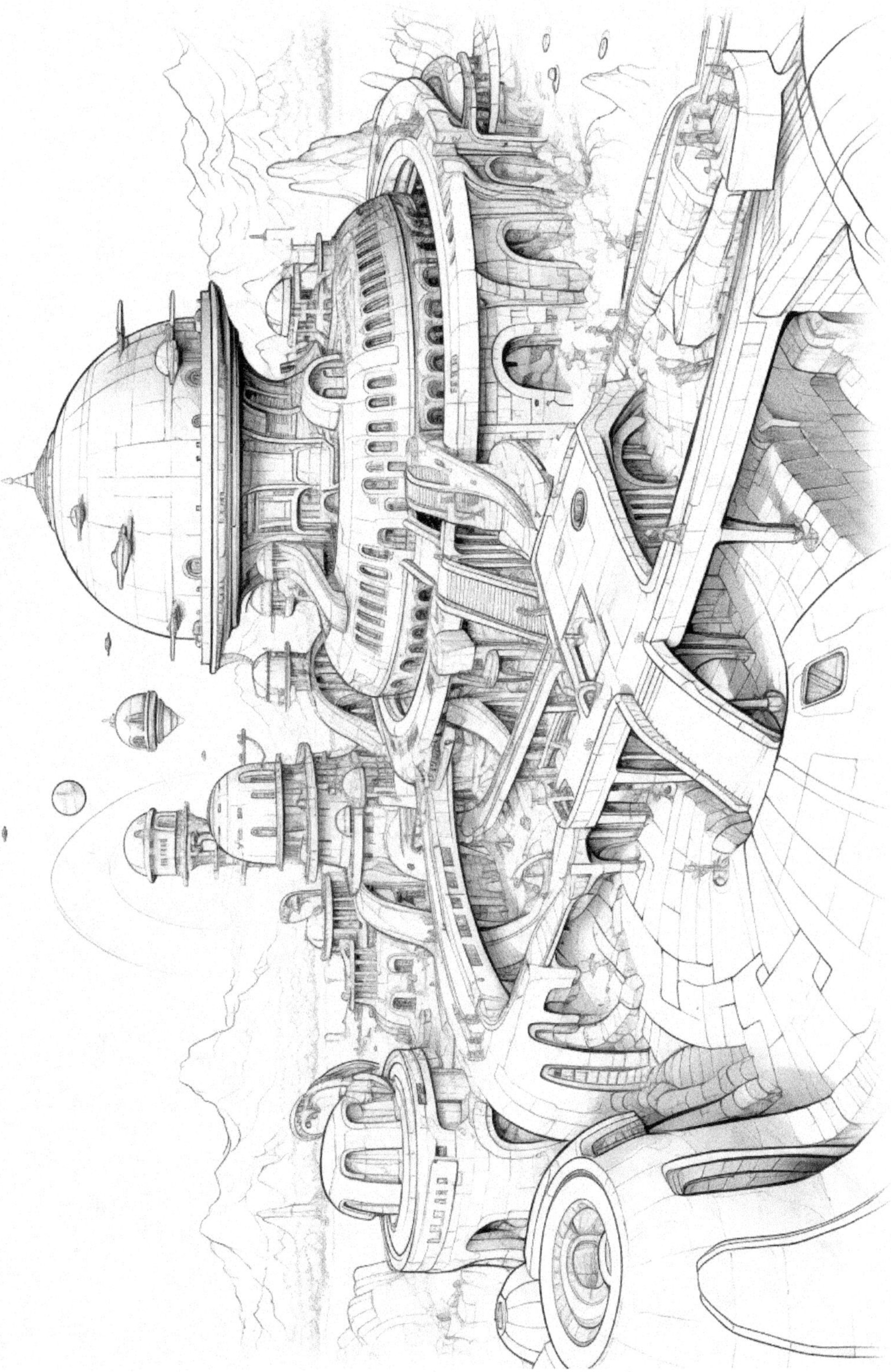

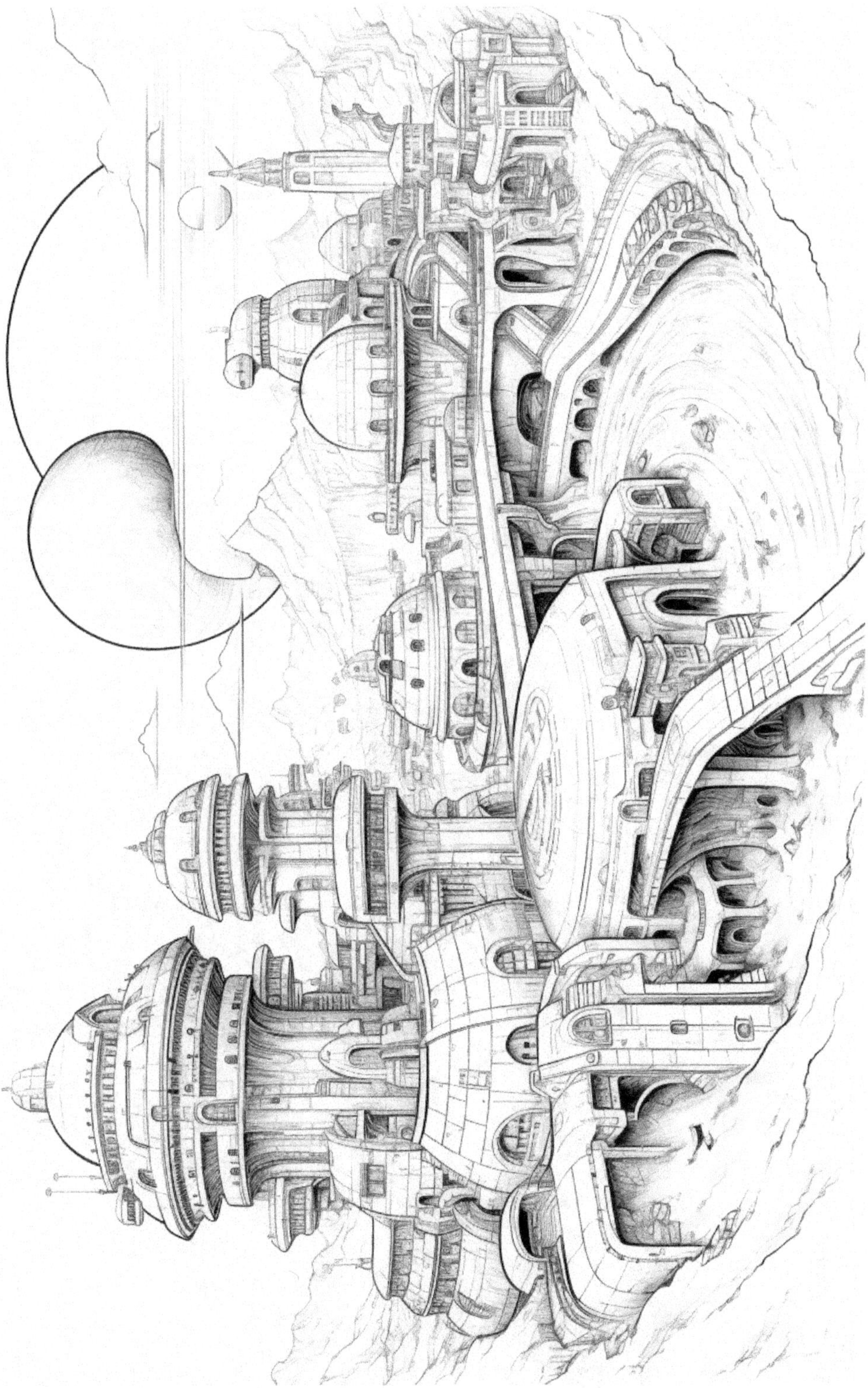

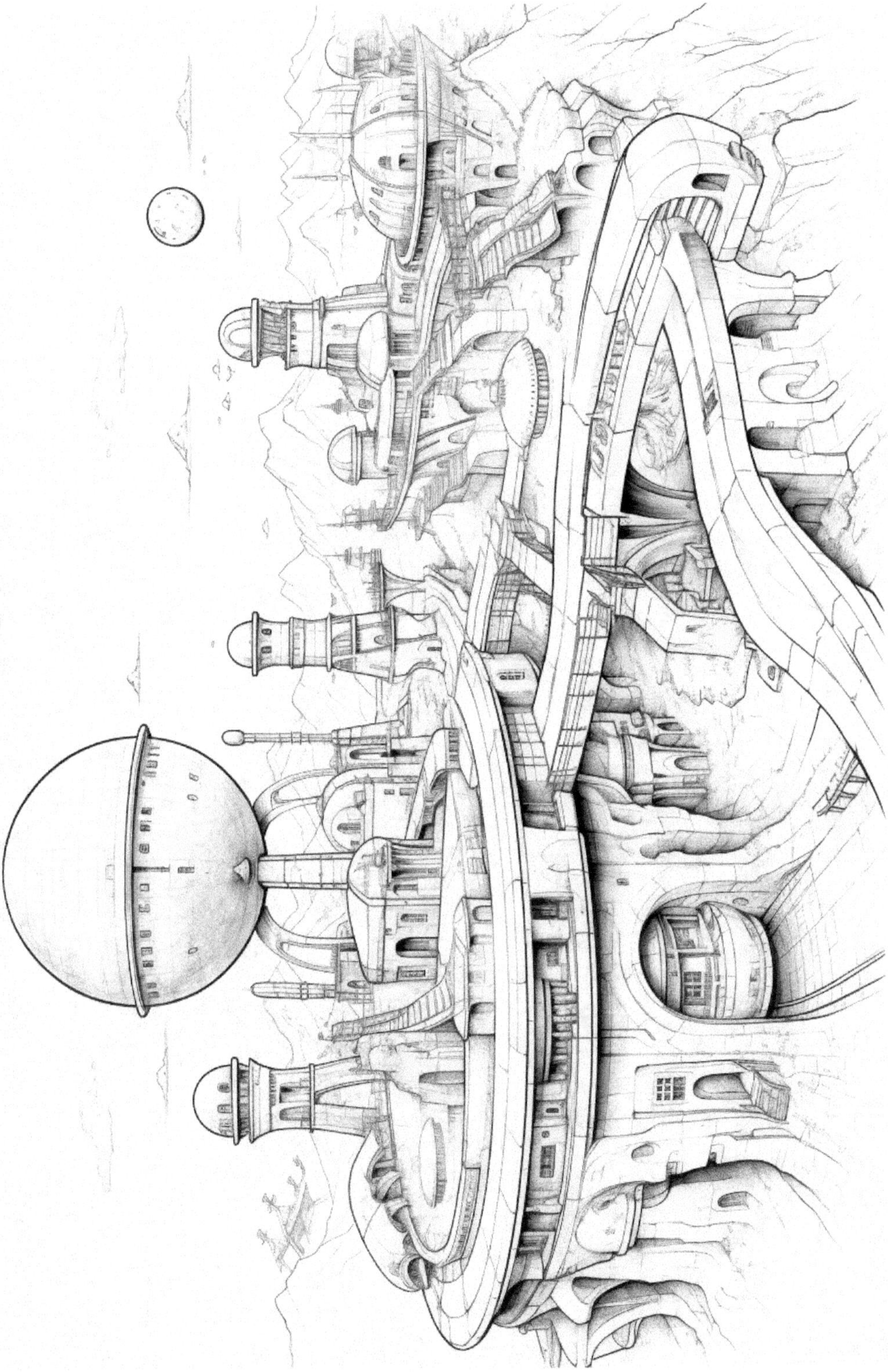

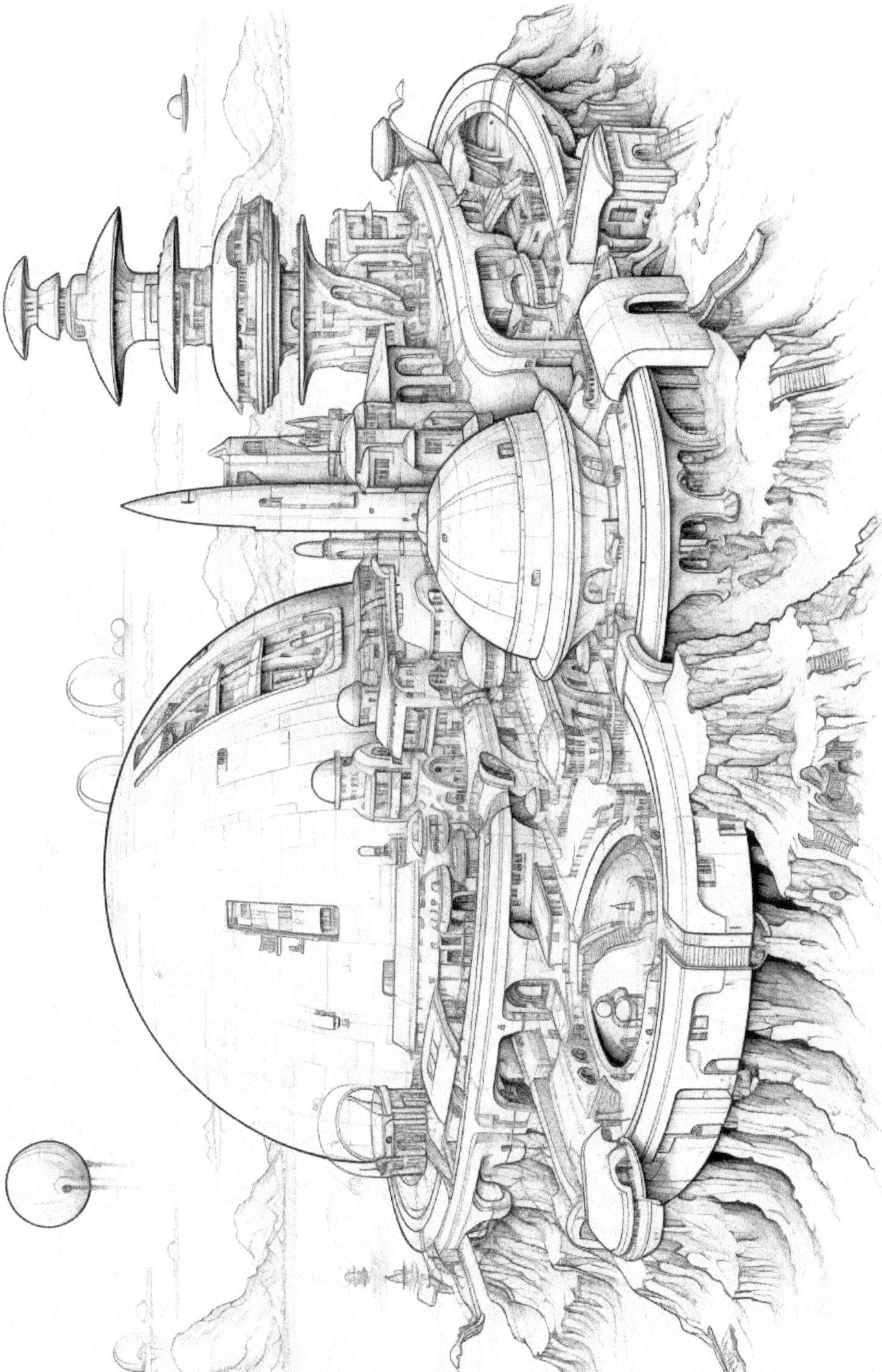

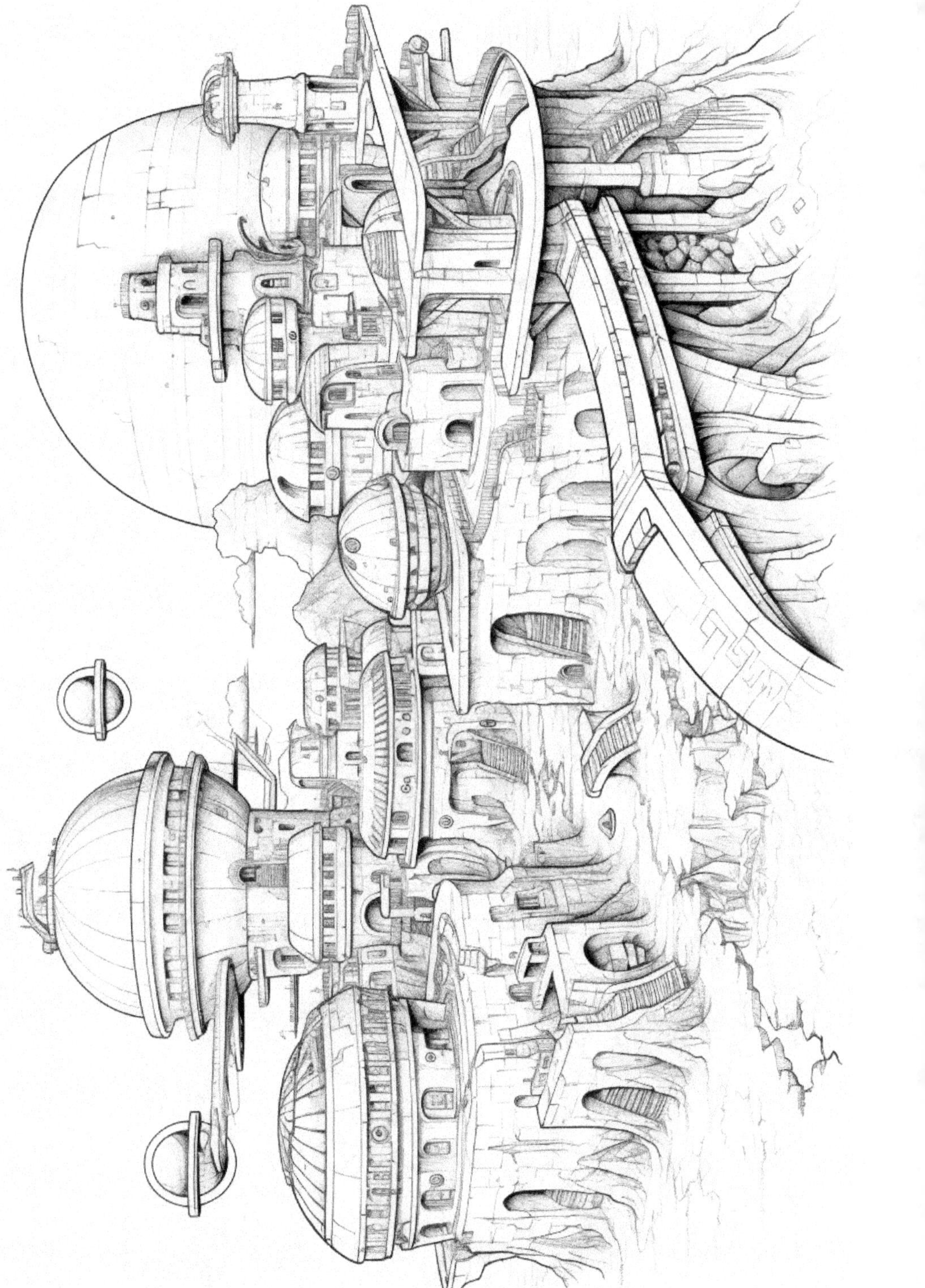

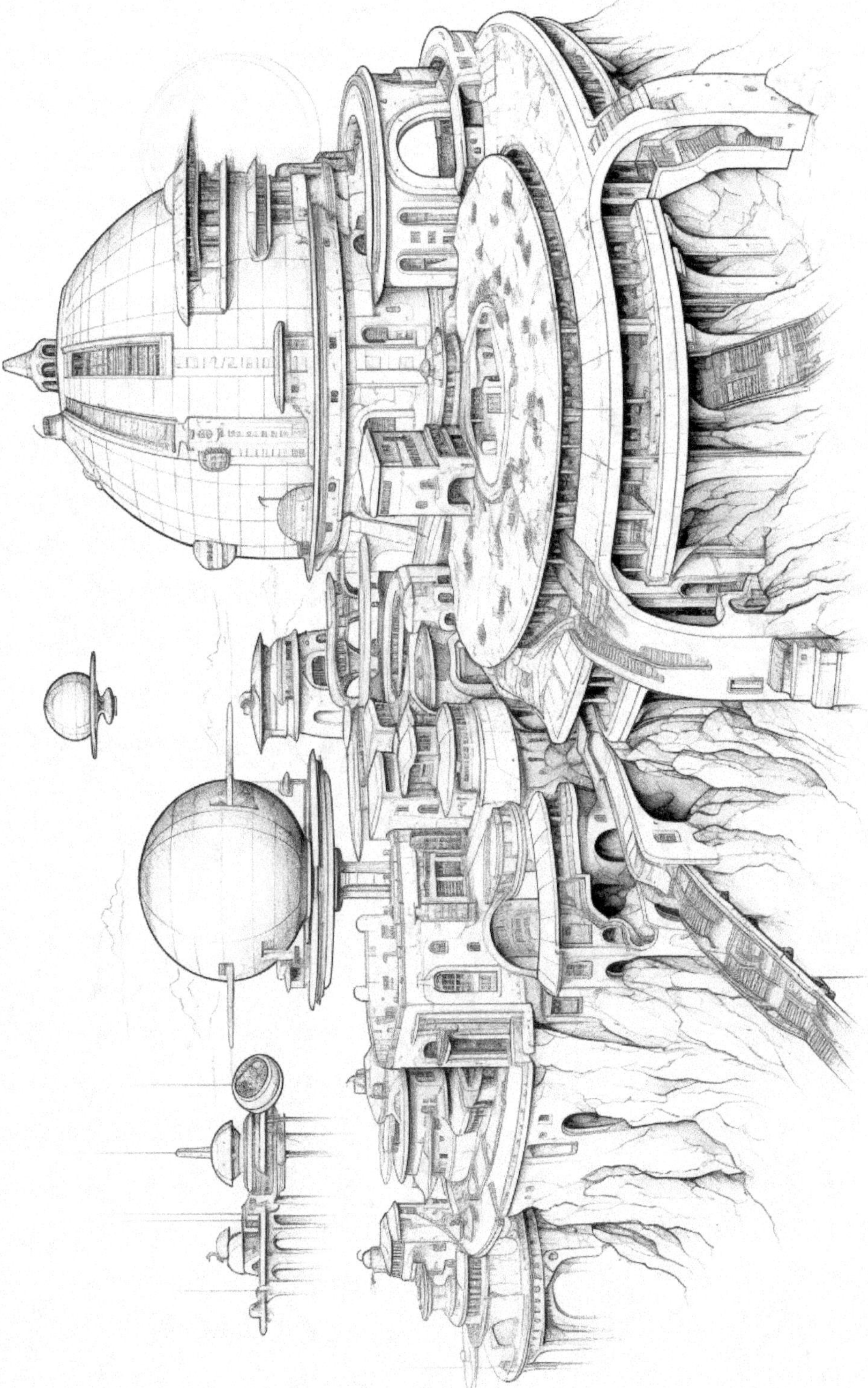

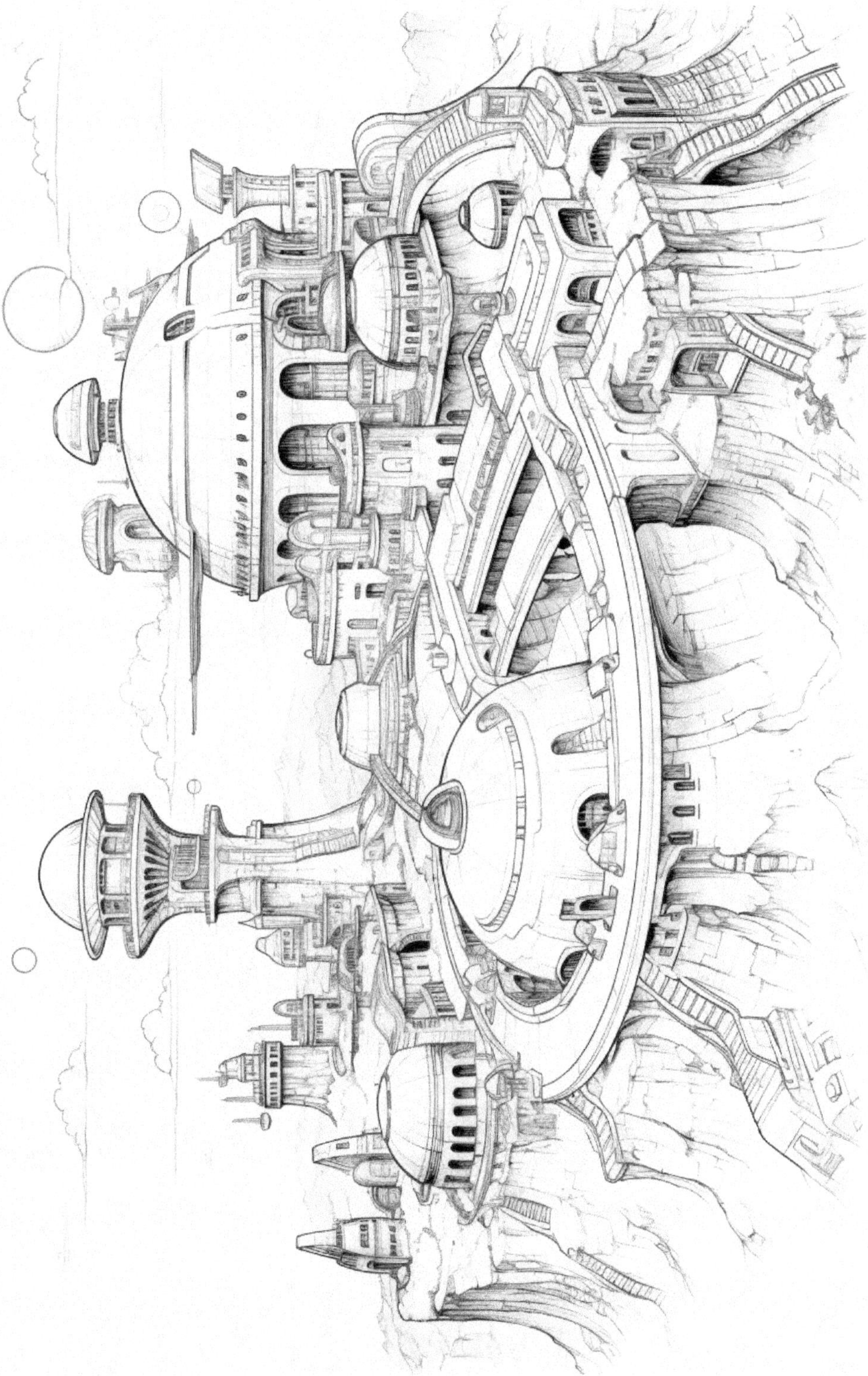

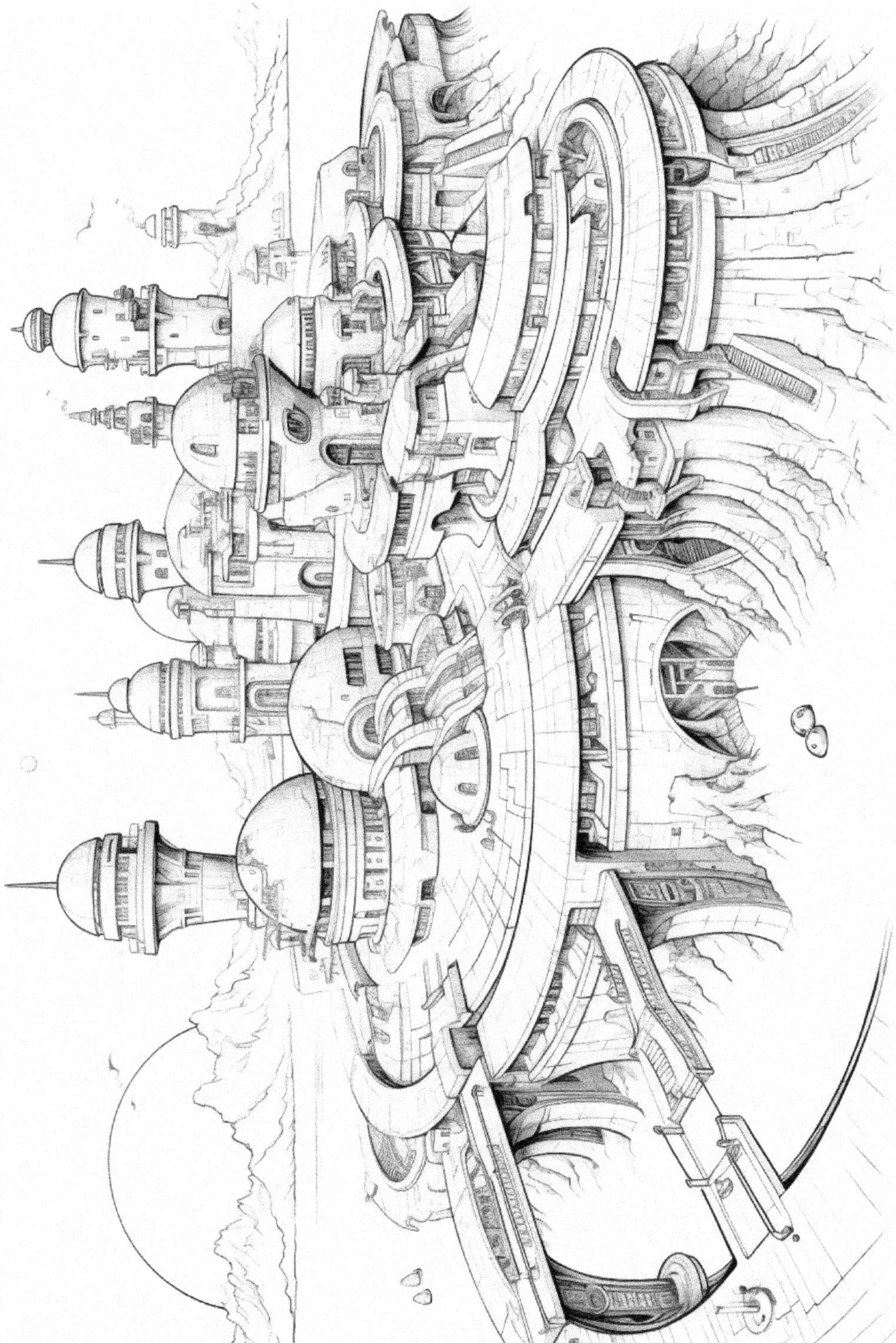

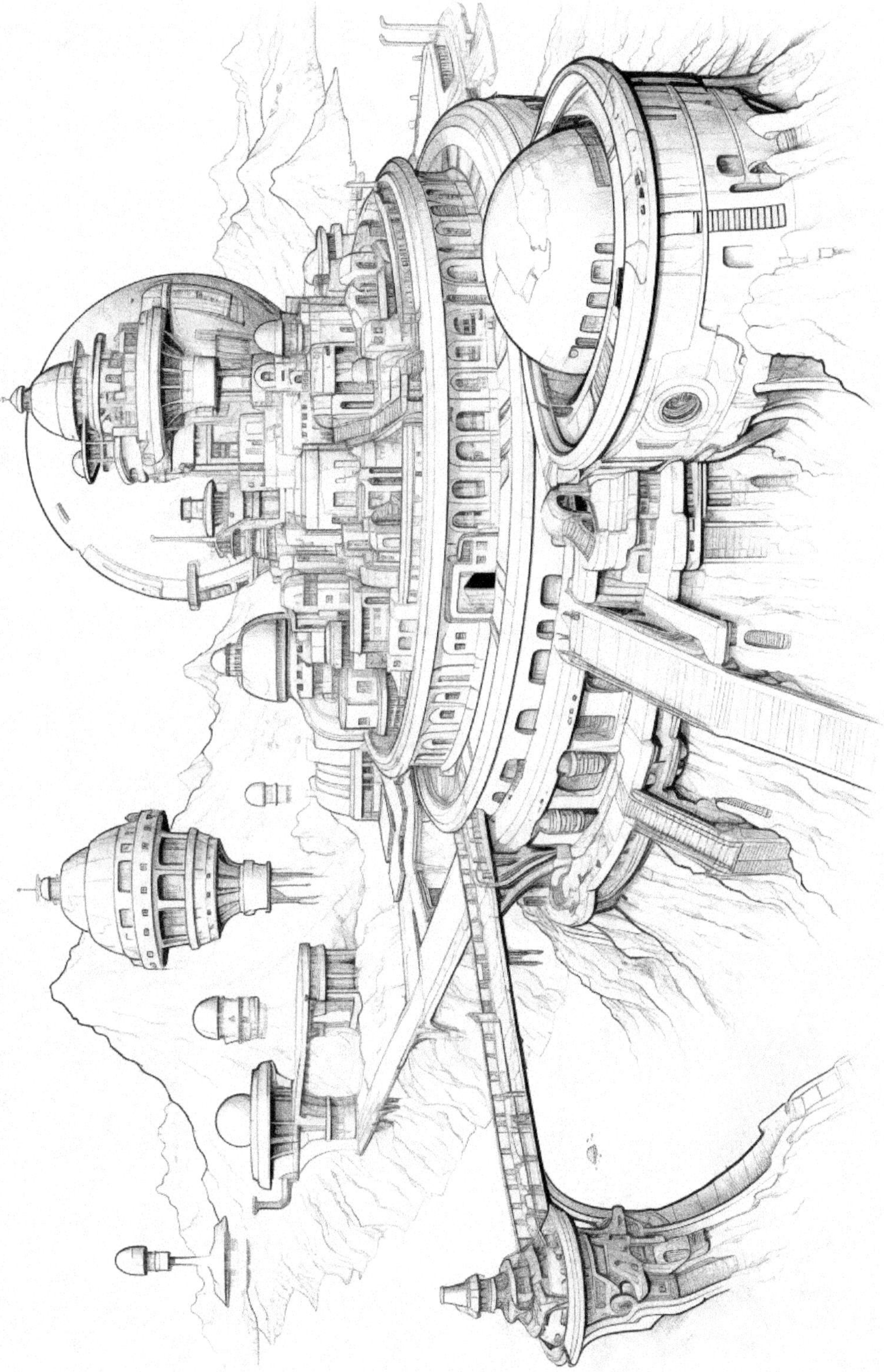

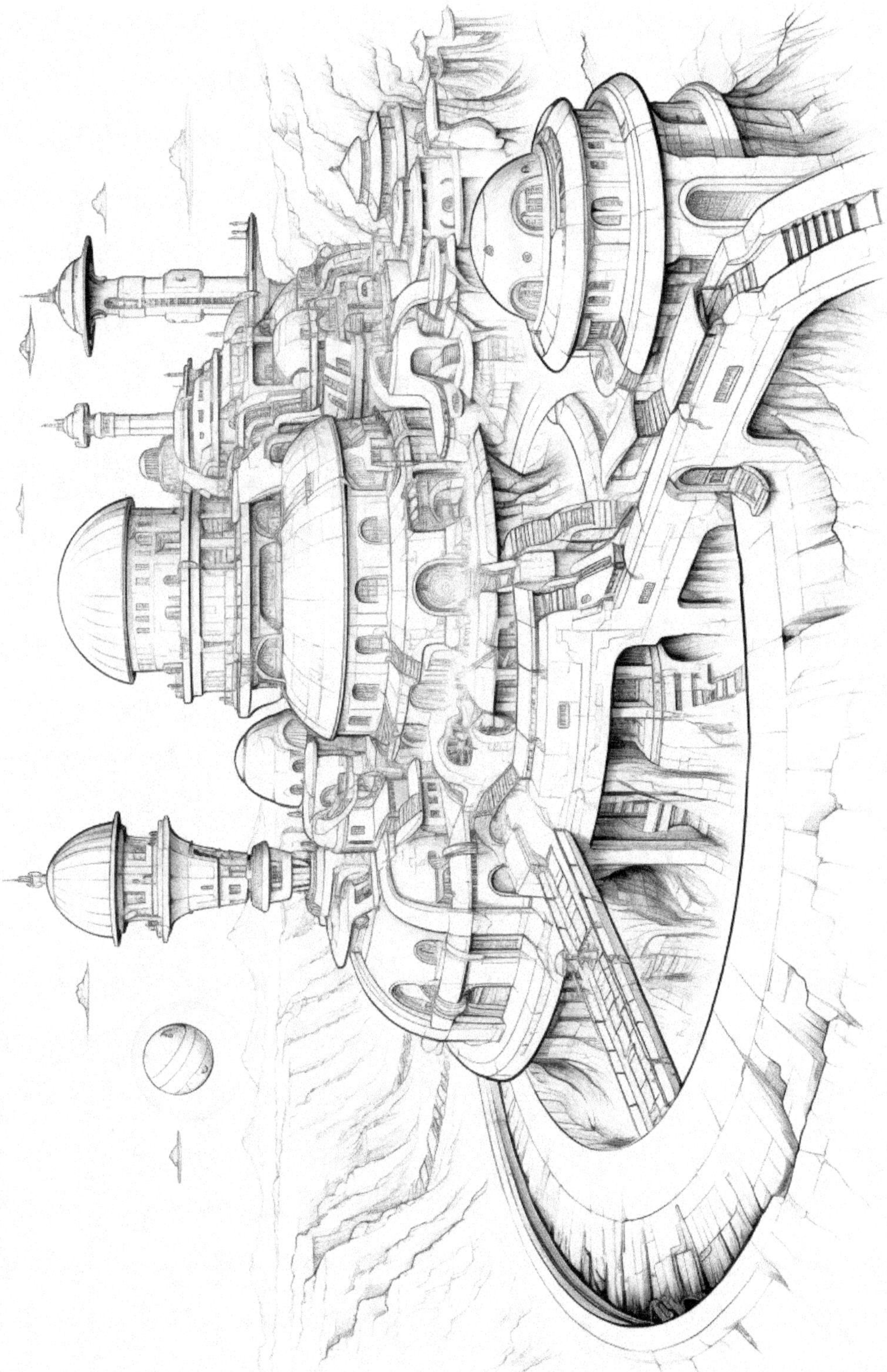

www.ingramcontent.com/pod-product-compliance
Lightning Source LLC
Chambersburg PA
CBHW062242290526
45794CB00006B/2368
9798856362168